THE A-Z OF CURIOUS
KENT

SUSAN McGOWAN

First published 2020

The History Press
97 St George's Place, Cheltenham,
Gloucestershire, GL50 3QB
www.thehistorypress.co.uk

British Library Cataloguing in Publication Data.
A catalogue record for this book is available from the British Library.

978 0 7509 9126 1

Typesetting and origination by The History Press
Printed and bound in Great Britain by TJ International Ltd.

Contents

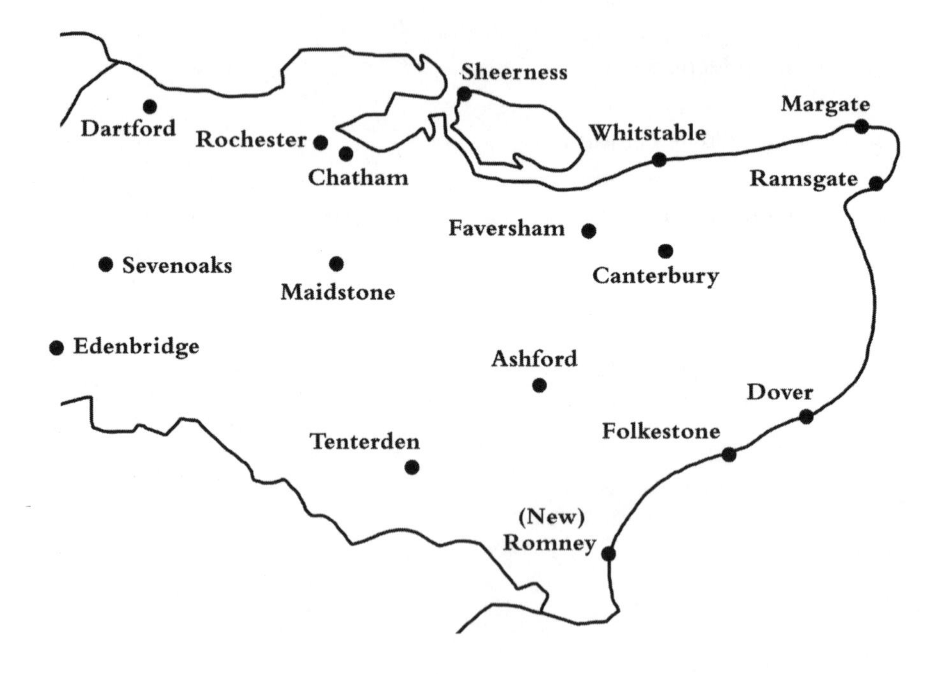
Sheerness
Margate
Dartford
Rochester
Whitstable
Chatham
Ramsgate
Faversham
Sevenoaks
Canterbury
Maidstone
Edenbridge
Ashford
Dover
Tenterden
Folkestone
(New)
Romney

Introduction

The first man to step onto British soil found himself in Kent, which makes this the oldest inhabited land in the country. For hundreds of thousands of years, man has lived, worked, loved and played on the slopes of the chalky Downs, in the rich forests and on the salt-flecked beaches. He has had time to reflect upon the nature of existence, come to terms with his mortality and look to the future. In doing so, the Men of Kent and the Kentish Men (and Maids!) have created a rich history, in legend and in fact.

We look to the future with our power stations and wind farms, but we also cling to many of our ancient customs and create new ones as we go.

Included in this book are just a few of the odd and fantastic stories about people and places in the county, reminding us that there are many, many things that cannot, and might never be, explained.

My particular thanks go to Christine Selby for her continued support and meticulous proofreading. As ever, all mistakes are my own.

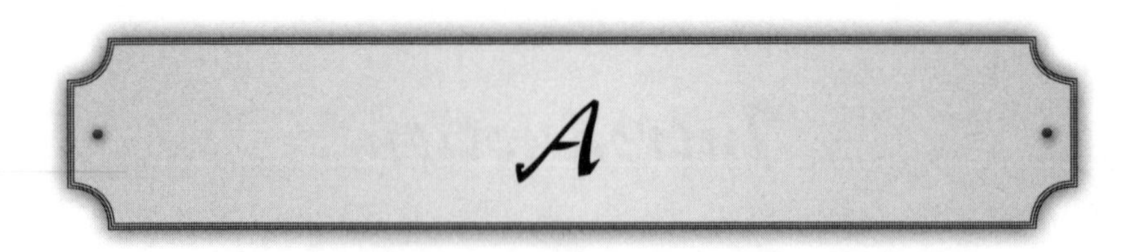

ALLUVIA: BODIES IN THE RIVER

An unwary tourist crossing the Westgate Bridge in Canterbury might be shocked to see two female figures submerged in the water. Depending on the time of day and the season of the year, the figures float serenely amongst the weeds and algae or glow eerily in the gloom.

Luckily, the figures are not the remains of murder or suicide, but are modern sculptures entitled *Alluvia*, created in cement and recycled glass resin by artist Jason deCaires Taylor. Referencing the painting of Ophelia by John Millais, the sculptures were installed in 2008 and draw continued interest from locals and visitors alike.

AMAZING ESCAPE AT THE METHODIST TEA: THE FATE OF A BELGIAN AEROPLANE

Nothing could have prepared the women who attended the Anniversary Tea at Sellindge Methodist Chapel on Wednesday, 1 June 1938 for the events of that afternoon. As the 100-strong group celebrated, they witnessed one of the most dramatic events in the history of the village. They heard the engine of an aeroplane overhead and then a terrible noise that sent shivers down their spines. A Belgian airliner had crashed into the roof of a house opposite and then into the chapel where they sat.

Amazingly, both the pilot and his radio operator – the only people on board – stepped out of the wreckage unhurt and joined the party, accepting refreshment from the stunned women of the group while they waited for assistance.

AMBER: THE FORGOTTEN GEM OF THE KENTISH SHORELINE

The graves of Saxon lords and ladies in Kent are littered with golden nuggets of amber, returning to the ground from whence they came. Amber is the fossilized resin of long-dead forests, taken by the sea and deposited on our coastline. Those pieces with a tiny portion of leaf or an insect captured inside are especially prized.

It is interesting to note that although the amber found in ancient graves is generally dark or red coloured, the amber found naturally occurring in Kentish soil is paler, with a distinctly yellowish tinge.

Once common in Thanet and along the north Kent coast, amber is now only rarely found on our shores, despite the fact that we have one of the longest coastlines of any county in the UK. Keep looking, though, and you may find a forgotten gem.

ARDEN OF FEVERSHAM: A LOST PLAY BY WILLIAM SHAKESPEARE

The play *Arden of Feversham* was written in 1592, and even after 500 years, nobody knows the name of the playwright. Many people think it was William Shakespeare, or was a collaboration between Shakespeare, Christopher Marlowe, and (possibly) other authors.

One thing is certain: Thomas Arden did live in Faversham, and was murdered by his wife and her lover. The crime happened in 1551, and it has been widely repeated in documents of the day and in books such as *The Newgate Calendar*, a work of 1795 which was the nineteenth-century equivalent of a docu-drama.

The plot of the play is simple, and faithfully follows the facts of the case: Alice Arden wanted to get rid of her husband so that she could marry her lover Richard Mosby. The events unfolded like a black comedy, with Arden refusing to drink the poisoned milk he was offered, and surviving a strangling attempt, a blow to the head and a cut throat, before he was repeatedly stabbed to death. Tales of a body concealed in a cupboard while guests were entertained nearby, a botched attempt to hide the corpse, and a trail of bloody footprints, make the whole affair seem like a farcical comedy sketch, but Arden was indeed murdered, and his killers were eventually brought to justice.

We know that Shakespeare often drew on historical stories for his plots, and London is not so far from Faversham. Perhaps he did collaborate with Kentish man Kit Marlowe, or with another playwright. Scholars point to the many linguistic similarities to Shakespeare's work, not least the reference to Alice Arden trying to scrub the blood from her floor: 'The blood cleaveth to the ground and will not out.' There is even a character called Shakebag in the play.

The killer of poor Thomas Arden was found, but unless further evidence comes to light, the author of the play *Arden of Feversham* may never be discovered.

ASHFORD'S TANK: A WAR MEMORIAL WITH A DIFFERENCE

It is curious to see the tank in Ashford, safe beneath a protective canopy and surrounded by shoppers, when her battle history was so brutal – it is a contrast that is hard to comprehend.

First World War tank in St George's Square, Ashford.

After the First World War, 200 towns across the UK were gifted with a tank to thank them for contributions given during the war. The Mark IV 'female' tank number 245 that is in St George's Square, Ashford, is now the only one of her type left in situ, as most were scrapped during the Second World War for their metal content. The tank at Ashford escaped destruction, as it housed the town's electricity transformer, having been stripped of its gearbox and fittings in 1929. It has now become a listed building and acts as a war memorial to those who died.

AUSTRALIA: HOME OF THE KENT BREWERY

Those who live in a quiet suburb just outside Sydney, Australia, may wonder why their gate still bears the Kentish county sign of the white horse rearing proudly, but it's not a mystery, just a matter of history.

Charles Newnham opened his brewery in Cranbrook in 1829, taking over as master brewer at the Baker's Cross Brewery and renaming it Newnham and Co., and later Newnham and Tooth, as his son-in-law joined him in the business. It was the Tooth family that had connections with Australia, and when Charles' daughter and her husband moved to Sydney, the Newnhams quickly followed.

By 1835, The Kent Brewery was up and running on the Parramatta Road, just outside the town, bringing to Australia their Kentish knowledge of hops and brewing. Gradually, the Tooth brothers and their descendants took over the day-to-day running of the brewery and in 1853 Charles returned to Kent.

The Kent Brewery had a lasting effect on the industry in Australia, as it was the first firm to introduce X, XX and XXX strength ratings on its products. Today, the Brisbane firm of Castlemaine offers a XXXX-rated beer, so when you pick up a can, remember that the easy identification of strength was introduced by men from Kent.

The building continued to be used as a brewery until 2005, but has now been redeveloped into housing.

B

BAT AND TRAP: AN EARLY FORM OF CRICKET

Bat and Trap is an east Kent pub game that is currently enjoying a bit of a revival, as pubs increase the number of games on offer to attract new customers in a disappearing market. This deceptively simple game is ideal for sunny pub gardens, and the source of much inter-village rivalry when played.

The 'trap' is a box containing a mechanical lever that throws the ball into the air so the batter can strike it with the side of his bat. As the ball comes out of the trap, the batter hits it along the 21-yard course, aiming for a narrow set of goalposts.

The team standing at the other end then choose a bowler to throw the ball back, aiming for the square flap in front of the trap – if he hits it, the player who hit the ball is out, if not, the batsman scores what is called a 'run', although no running is involved.

It is easy to see how this could have developed into the game of cricket.

BATTLE OF BOSSENDEN WOOD: THE LAST TRUE BATTLE ON ENGLISH SOIL

The Battle of Bossenden Wood took place on 31 May 1838 near Hernhill in Kent and has been called the last true battle on English soil.

The battle was fought by a small group of labourers from Hernhill, Dunkirk and Boughton against a detachment of over 100 soldiers from the 45th Regiment of Foot, stationed at Canterbury. Their leader, a man who called himself Sir William Percy Honeywood Courtenay, Knight of Malta, was actually John Nichols Thom, from Cornwall, who had spent five years in Barming Heath Lunatic Asylum and now declared himself to be Christ returned.

In the days that led up to the battle, a growing number of people had engaged in boisterous but not riotous behaviour, rallying under Courtney's promise of bread and free land for all. Many may also have been swayed by his threats of fire and brimstone for those who deserted him.

On Sunday, 27 May, Thom marched from Graveney, through Dargate and on to Bossenden, by which time he had gathered forty followers. The local constable, Nicholas Mears, his brother, and one other man were sent to arrest Courtenay, but Nicholas was shot and the other two escaped to find help

Thom fell back to Waterham, but the next day he and his followers made their way toward Bossenden again, where they were met by 100 men of the 45th, led by Major Armstrong. When the two forces met, Major Armstrong read the Riot Act, much as an individual is read his Miranda Rights today. Thom and his gang did not disperse and shots were exchanged.

The names of those involved in the Battle of Bossenden Wood.

Eleven men lost their lives in the brief confrontation: Courtenay, eight of his followers and two of those sent to apprehend them. At the assizes that followed, most of Courtenay's band was discharged as it was deemed they had been 'led astray' by Courtenay, although three were sentenced to be transported.

Soon afterwards, Dunkirk church and school were built to rectify what was seen as a lack of moral guidance in the area, which may be the most remarkable thing of all about this sorry tale.

THE BATTLE OF SANDWICH: AN INVASION BY THE FRENCH IS NARROWLY DEFEATED

St Bartholomew's Day, 24 August, is remembered in East Kent as the anniversary of the Battle of Sandwich, for it was on this day that England was invaded by the French.

In 1216, when King John looked likely to renege on the terms of the Magna Carta, a group of English barons decided to invite the French Dauphin, Louis, to come to England as an alternative monarch to John's young son Henry III. After a bloody eighteen months, during which Louis hung on to the crown by the skin of his teeth (*see* King Louis of England), Louis retreated to France to regroup, before returning to England to take the throne once and for all.

Louis' troops arrived at Sandwich in 1217, sacked what they could find, burnt the rest and waited for reinforcements before sailing on to London, where they would join Louis. The plucky men of Sandwich, under one Stephen Crabbe, launched the ragged remainder of their fleet and attacked the waiting French ships, led by Eustace the Monk, a notorious pirate.

Legend has it that as the ships approached, Eustace's ship seemed to disappear, but Stephen was not fooled. He had about him an ancient piece of blue glass, through which he squinted. The Sandwich fleet continued the battle as Stephen ordered his crew to sail towards what appeared to be open water. They did so, wondering that he kept the piece of glass to his eye. Shortly, the ship shuddered as if it had hit a sandbank and Stephen swung his sword. Immediately, a ghostly ship appeared, along with the severed head of Eustace the Monk.

Serious historians will give you details of the number of men and the size of the fleet, and assert that Eustace was, in fact, discovered hiding in the hold of his ship when it was taken. They will also tell you that the disappearance of the ships was caused by the use of barrels of quicklime, which had been catapulted at the French ships and blinded soldiers on both sides of the fight. Whatever the truth of the story, the men of Sandwich had won the day and Louis never did gain full control of the English crown.

In memory of the event, the town built a chapel and a row of almshouses in St Bartholomew's name, now known locally as St Bart's Hospital.

A further legacy of the battle is the Bun Run, held annually, during which the children of the town run around the church and are rewarded with a currant bun. Adults are offered a biscuit with the date 1190 imprinted upon it, as the supposed founding of the hospital – just another anomaly in the story of the Battle of Sandwich.

BAXTERS: A SPECIAL SHOE FOR SHINGLE BEACHES

We know that fishermen and farmers wear specialised clothing to protect themselves from the elements, but this special type of shoe is rather unusual.

The beaches of Dungeness are made of shingle, built up by years of longshore drift, and are difficult to walk on. Pathways and roads have now been cut across the landscape, but in the days before these had been created, local people got over the difficulty by wearing backstays or baxters. These were pieces of wood about 50cm long and 15cm wide attached to the shoe by a strap of leather, rather like a snow shoe, so the wearers could slide across the top of the stones without sinking.

Charles Igglesden, writing in 1905, describes the shoes and tells us that cart wheels were similarly encased in wood so they could be pulled across the shingle like a sled. To see several people skating over the top of a dry beach must have been an incredible sight to behold.

BEACH FLAME BARRAGE: WE WILL FIGHT THEM ON THE BEACHES

It is only recently that details of plans to defend the country against an invasion by the German army have been released. Men in specialist divisions have kept their secrets, and the particulars about sabotage and guerrilla tactics have remained hidden. Kent, of course, was the front line of this defence.

The Petroleum Warfare Department was created in 1940 in response to fears that an invasion by the German military could be possible. Following investigations into a Sea Flame Barrage, whereby oil was floated on the sea and ignited, forming an impassable barrier, the department soon realised that a flame barrage on land was, in fact, more stable and easier to control. In 1941, therefore, a series of Beach Flame Barrages were set up along the south coast.

Tanks of fuel were sited at regular intervals along the eastern coast of the county, buried in shingle beaches or soft earth, hidden from German aircraft reconnaissance. Each tank had a pipe leading out onto the beach and was controlled from a pumping station or control post.

As there was no German invasion, the system was never put into use, but every now and then historians find remnants of the system, such as an overgrown pumping station or, as in the case of The Clarendon Hotel in Deal, equipment left in a cellar.

THE BEAST OF TUNBRIDGE WELLS: THE LOCAL YETI STILL STALKS THE STREETS

Much has been written about the Beast of Tunbridge Wells, or the Apeman of Tunbridge Wells or even the Bigfoot of Tunbridge Wells, but the consensus of opinion is that those who have been unfortunate enough to see the beast are victims of a prank.

The first sighting was in 1942, and regular sightings over the years have developed the creature into an 8ft-tall hirsute Neanderthal, incapable of speech, but with burning eyes.

Many people think it is a hoax, and yet with no concrete evidence either way, an equal number of people believe the beast still roams the countryside. The truth of its existence has still to be discovered.

BEATING OF THE BOUNDS OF THE RIVER MEDWAY: AN AGE-OLD CUSTOM STILL IN PLACE

Beating the Bounds of the parish is not a custom that is restricted to the county of Kent, and yet you will not find another like this in the whole of England.

In days gone by, children and newcomers were required to join their neighbours in an annual procession around the bounds of the parish, beating the path with a willow stick. In the days before written records, this was a useful way of teaching children where the boundaries lay, and usually took place on Rogation Day, on 25 April. Some villages in Kent still uphold the tradition, but it is getting less and less widespread.

A more unusual custom is the annual cruise of the River Medway in June each year, which performs the same function as those who Beat the Bounds on land.

The custom goes back to the time of Henry VI, who granted a Charter to the City of Rochester, by which the Mayor of Rochester was also granted the title 'Admiral of the Waters of The River Medway from Sherenesse to Hawkewode'. Each year, the Admiral travels from Rochester Pier, up the Medway to the Hawkwood Stone, where a cannon shot is fired and the barge turns. The entourage then travels back down to Garrison Point, stopping to lay a wreath at the spot where HMS *Bulwark* was destroyed in 1914. Another cannon shot is fired at the furthest reaches of the bounds.

The event is growing in popularity, and is now staged over two consecutive days. Up to seventy fishing boats and yachts can be seen during the ceremony, which is organised by the Rochester Oyster and Floating Fishery, an ancient order established in the sixteenth century, to organise and police the river.

THE BELLS, THE BELLS! TALES FROM ACROSS THE COUNTY

Coming through!

On Bluebell Hill, between Maidstone and Rochester, there were once two pubs, called the Upper Bell and Lower Bell, one at each end of the hill. Many years ago, the road was too narrow for horse and coach teams to pass each other, so a bell was rung at either pub when a coach was about to depart, to warn those at the other end. Simple, but effective. Today, only the Lower Bell is still operating as a pub.

The church bell of St Nicholas church in Barfreston.

An Outside Bell

Further to the east, the Norman church of St Nicholas at Barfreston is noteworthy for its intricately carved Caen stone walls, unlike any other in the county. It is also remarkable for the fact that although it has a bell, it has no bell tower. The bell is hung outside the church in a yew tree. A gibbet-like frame has been constructed, from which the bell hangs, and which is still in use today, rung from inside the church.

A Conical Tower

Visitors to the Romney Marsh area are startled to see the steeple of Brookland church, which stands separate from the main body of the building. Built of wood, in a conical design, the steeple has the shape of three cones of descending sizes topped by a weathervane. It seems that the addition of a traditional tower would have been too heavy for the little church, which stands on soft, marshy ground.

Despite this logical explanation, many local legends have grown up around the tower, including the assertion that the tower jumped off the top of the church in surprise when an unlikely couple came to be married, or that it was blown off during a particularly violent storm.

The structure has been dated to 1260 and is in fact a bell cage rather than a tower, with the bells suspended directly from the wooden frame. The current shape evolved when the height of the tower was increased in the fifteenth century. The weathervane on top of the tower is in itself notable, as it depicts a dragon and not the usual farm animal or religious symbol.

A Set of Secular Bells

On a clear day, just outside Birchington, one can hear bells ringing out over the Kent countryside where there is no church to be seen. One of only a few sets of secular bells, known as a 'peal', the twelve bells are rung from Quex House. The bells are housed in the Waterloo Tower, constructed from brick and cast iron by John Powell to celebrate the country's victory over Napoleon. The family name is now Powell-Cotton, but they still own the house and the bells are rung by the Quex Society of Change Ringers.

BENJAMIN BEALE: PROPONENT OF THE GREAT BRITISH SEASIDE

At the beginning of the eighteenth century, swimming in the sea was the pursuit of none but the hardiest males. It was much safer, and fully recommended by doctors of the day, to drink seawater rather than bathe in it. So why did it change, and why was it a Kentish man that changed it?

As the century progressed, more and more people started to visit seaside towns such as Margate, hoping for some relaxation and possibly a cure for their ailments. Many even took to bathing, but the sexes were strictly segregated, with the women bathing close to the seashore, while the men were rowed out to deeper waters before they could dive in.

One of the problems with bathing at Margate was the shallowness of the water – bathers had to walk out a long way before their modesty could be hidden by the waves.

Towards the middle of the century, Margate Quaker, one-time draper and entrepreneur, Benjamin Beale, started to produce and hire out the first bathing machines seen in Britain. Consisting at its most basic of a covered wagon pulled by a horse, shy bathers could wait in the wagon until the horse had been driven into the water. A full canopy was lowered like a tent over the whole wagon, the bather could descend into the sea via a set of steps without being seen until they were modestly submerged and thus ladies could bathe inside the tented area in total privacy.

Without a patent, the idea was soon copied at other resorts and quickly became commonplace. Postcards of the day show rows of bathing machines lined up on beaches all around the UK. Beale received little recompense apart from the pennies paid by his customers and is today all but forgotten.

BERT TURNER: AN FA FIRST

Herbert Turner was known as Bert to his friends, and played football for Charlton Athletic. He was 35 at the time of the 1946 FA Cup Final, and became the first player in the history of the game to score for both sides. First, he knocked the ball into his own goal while trying to kick it out of the way, but within minutes he went on to score for his own side. What a way to become famous!

Although born in Wales and proud to be a Welshman, Bert later took over the Jolly Farmer in Manston and spent many happy years there, running the pub from 1957 until 1980.

BETHERSDEN MARBLE: AS FINE A STONE AS ANY IN THE COUNTRY

A monument to the Roper family made of Bethersden marble.

Once highly sought after, marble from Bethersden appears in both Rochester and Canterbury Cathedrals. The colours in the limestone range from brown to blue and come from the fossilised shells of the freshwater snail.

Despite the name, the stone is quarried across Kent, and most examples are found outside the Bethersden area; it can be seen on both the church and pavements of Biddenden, for example. 'Marble' is a term applied to a stone that can be highly polished, and Bethersden marble has been used to create the font at the church of St John the Baptist at Harrietsham. Unfortunately, the stone doesn't hold the shine, quickly becoming dull, and its use was soon abandoned.

The stone was also used to pave the roads of West Kent, and the hard-wearing quality of these byways contributed to the rise of Wealden industries, enabling easy import of materials and export of finished goods.

BIG CATS: AT NIGHT, WE ARE NOT ALONE

The fear of big cats in the countryside has taken over from the ancient fear of wolves in the forest, or highwaymen on the road. The possibility of something like a big cat lurking dangerously near adds a frisson of excitement to life, although the reality is not so pleasant.

The evidence for big cats in the Kent countryside is strong. Multiple sightings along with evidence of animal kills make it probable that several big cats do live in the woods around us. What size and type they are, however, is hard to determine.

Livestock, from sheep to deer, are regularly although not frequently killed, and the reports originate from all over the county, from Sheppey to Romney Marsh and Thanet to the Weald of Kent. Big cats have been seen in open spaces, wooded areas, on roads and in fields. The marks on an animal mauled by a big cat are distinctly different from those on a carcase attacked by a dog, even a large one, and are easily recognised by vets and farmers.

Sightings run to over ten a year, and with anecdotal evidence piling up, there can be no doubt about the existence of these animals, watching and waiting in the woodlands around us.

BISHOP'S FINGER: NOT WHAT YOU THINK

The bishop's finger, cause of so much schoolboy hilarity, is the local name for the finger-like signposts that show the route along the Pilgrims Way from Winchester to Thomas à Becket's tomb in Canterbury. It is also known as a pointing post.

They are hard to find nowadays, much like the signpost on the road out of Finglesham that points the way to the nearby village of Ham and the town of Sandwich. The sign reads 'Ham Sandwich' and has become something of a local landmark.

The Bishop's Finger alehouse in Canterbury.

The famous 'Ham Sandwich' road sign.

BLACK ROBES FOR THE MAYOR OF SANDWICH: A REMINDER OF A TERRIBLE EVENT

The Mayor of Sandwich, on the most eastern coast of Kent, always wears black robes. This is in memory of a past holder of the office, John Drury, who lost his life in 1457 when the French attacked the town.

At the time, Sandwich was a thriving medieval port and as such was an attractive target for the 4,000-strong army under Marshal of France, Pierre de Breze. The townsmen were eventually relieved by reinforcements from other Cinque Ports, but the town was destroyed and many, including the mayor, lost their lives.

As part of his regalia, the Mayor also carries a blackthorn wand, to ward off evil spirits and witches – a little bit of pagan folklore that has survived to the present day. One might say that this is unnecessary in modern society, but who knows what disasters have been averted because of the presence of that wand.

THE BLACK ROBIN: HERO OR VILLAIN?

'Black robin' was a local term for highwaymen who, although feared by those with money, were seen as heroes by many working folk. Historically, Essex had the most highwaymen operating within its boundaries, but Kent came a close second. The Black Robin pub in Kingston, just south of Canterbury, is named after a local highwayman known as the Black Robber or Black Robin.

The fear of highwaymen attacking a traveller on foot or in a coach has left a mark on our countryside. Roads that passed through wooded areas were widened to leave an open sward of scrubland on each side, to minimise the risk of a surprise attack from the forest.

Fear of the highwayman was, however, mainly a problem of the rich; poorer people admired their courage and cunning, and many highwaymen became local celebrities. Those highwaymen who were caught were hanged for their crimes, ending their lives on Penenden Heath gallows, and several, like Elias Shepherd, who was hanged there in 1765, continue to roam the Kent countryside as ghosts.

Hero or villain – you decide.

BLESSINGS OF LAND AND SEA: A PRAYER FOR A BOUNTIFUL HARVEST

Almost every coastal town with a fishing industry has a Blessing of the Seas ceremony, but the one at Margate is slightly different from the rest. Presided over by members of the Greek Orthodox clergy, the ceremony is held on 6 January, Epiphany, the day Jesus was baptised in the River Jordan.

After a service at the nearby church, the Bishop is accompanied to the harbour by visiting dignitaries, where they throw a floral crucifix into the sea. The offering is retrieved by a boy, conscious of the honour bestowed upon him, who is presented with the cross as thanks for his bravery.

The blessing of the land might have seemed too pagan a ritual for early clerics, and they chose instead to bless the plough, symbol of the labours of man, rather than the land itself. The blessings took place on Plough Sunday, in January, and it is a custom that persists in All Saints' Church, Staplehurst, where a horse-drawn plough is brought into the church for the ceremony.

BLOOR'S COACH RIDES AT MIDNIGHT: A HEADLESS GHOST RACES THROUGH THE COUNTRY LANES

This is a ghost story that has everything: a jilted lover, a bloody murder and a headless ghost.

Bloor's coach is a ghostly apparition that can be seen in Rainham travelling between the church and Berengrave Lane, eventually ending up at Bloor's Place, where it mysteriously disappears.

The coach, with its headless horses and its headless coachman and footman, is said to carry Christopher Bloor, who travels with his head under his arm.

When he was alive, Bloor so enraged the men of Rainham with his constant attention to their wives that they waylaid him one evening and cut off his head. The head was mounted on a spike and raised to the top of Rainham church, where it stayed until the morning.

The coach travels from the church, past the place where he lost his life, and on to the home he shared with his wife, Agnes, only stopping for water at Queen Court. The coach is often accompanied by the sound of Agnes' sobbing.

The coach is said to travel nightly, so perhaps you can see it yourself if you are in the area when the clock strikes twelve.

BLUE DICK CULMER: A MOST UN-CHRISTIAN CHRISTIAN

The Most Reverand 'Blue Dick' Culmer gained his nickname not from his colourful language, but from the colour of his clothing. Avoiding the traditional black robes of the priesthood, he took to wearing blue cloth, and it certainly made him memorable. His first post, in 1630, was at Goodnestone, but he held several clerical posts throughout Kent during his lifetime.

He was supposedly despised by his parishioners for his zealous application of the laws of the Church, and after being central to the sacking of Canterbury Cathedral after the English Civil War, during which he destroyed many priceless 'idolatrous monuments', his reputation worsened.

He was denied entry to his new parish at Minster-in-Thanet when he went to take up the appointment. The people of the parish attacked him, bribed him and wrote to the Crown about him, and he eventually moved away to Monkton, where he lived until his death. All evidence points to the fact that he was disliked by all with whom he came in contact, apart from, perhaps, his immediate family, although maybe I am being too kind.

BODYSNATCHERS: A NECESSARY EVIL

Any person passing through a graveyard at night is bound to feel a frisson of excitement or a tremor of fear. Tales of ghosts and the dead rising from their graves are commonplace, but in this day and age we don't really expect to see an open grave as we pass by. A hundred years ago, however, the prospect of seeing an empty grave was entirely possible, although the likelihood that the inhabitant had clawed his or her way out was remote.

During the nineteenth century, the sharp rise in medical knowledge was made possible by a regular supply of corpses for dissection and study. Most of the reputable hospitals who undertook this work were based in London, and the temptation to provide bodies with no questions asked was strong in the Home Counties.

The problem of obtaining enough corpses for the medical students stemmed from the fact that it was illegal to cut up human flesh; only the bodies of those legally executed for murder or treason could be used. This pushed up the value of a corpse brought to the hospital 'no questions asked' to an amazing £25, an amount equivalent to approximately £3,000 today.

By the mid-nineteenth century, the supply of legal corpses was so low that the Home Secretary directed the police to turn a blind eye to the transport of bodies, and the ease of transferring goods into London by boat made Kent a hotbed of activity for those who became known as 'the resurrection men'. The bodies needed to be as fresh as possible if they were to be of use as an educational tool, and the graves of those newly dead were at serious risk. Grieving relatives were forced to employ people to watch over the graves of the recently departed to ensure they remained where they had been placed.

The Anatomy Act, passed in 1832, finally allowed students to dissect the body of any person, with the permission of their relatives, and this largely put an end to the gruesome trade of bodysnatching.

BOILS AND CARBUNCLES: NO MAN IS SAFE

In the mid-nineteenth century, even the best medical thinking of the day couldn't save one of the best philosophical thinkers of the day.

Poor Karl Marx, that eminent German philosopher, was plagued with persistent and painful boils, which lowered his mood and often prevented him from working. When he lived in London, he came to stay in Kent several times, both at Ramsgate and Margate, although he was disappointed with Canterbury, which seemed to him a run-down place.

In 1866, when he was approaching his 50th birthday, he stayed at the Royal Sea Bathing Hospital in Margate for several weeks, which offered him some relief, but the boils, which have now been identified as part of a chronic skin condition, sadly returned soon afterwards.

BREAD DOLES AND ALMSHOUSES: CHARITABLE DONATIONS FROM WILLS AND BEQUESTS

In the days before the Welfare State introduced a national system of benefits for the poor, those in need relied solely on local benefactors to provide help when they were unemployed or elderly. Many people placed money in trust for the benefit of the poor, and although almost all have been amalgamated, some still run independently.

An example of such a trust is that given in the will of William Hayes. In 1678, he left a sum of money to pay for a donation of bread to the poor of the parish of Cobham each Christmas Eve 'for ever'.

Much has been written about the Biddenden Maids, Eliza and Mary Chulkhurst, conjoined twins who donated alms to the poor after a life of piety and prayer. When Mary died, aged 34, Eliza refused to be separated from her, and died soon afterwards, lending poignancy to the story, but historical researchers dispute not only the details of the case, but also whether Mary and Eliza ever existed at all.

The money was originally used to pay for 'The Biddenden Dole', a gift of bread and cheese to the poor. The lands supposedly donated by the sisters has now been sold for housing, but the money raised, and the interest therefrom, supplemented by sales of Biddenden Cakes, still pays for an annual gift to the poor of the parish, given out each Easter Monday.

In his book, *A Collection of Old English Customs: And Curious Bequests and Charities*, Henry Edwards reports that Salmstone Grange in the parish of St John's in Margate was leased on the understanding that, in the first and third weeks of Lent, the lessee should give out to twenty-four people in Thanet nine loaves of bread and eighteen herrings. He was further required to distribute six ells (about 3 yards) of blankets, and also, from May to June, give every poor person who came to Salmstone Grange a dish of peas. However, it was noted that at the time of writing, in 1842, although the bread was still given out, 6*d* (six old pence) was given in lieu of the herrings, and that the distribution of peas had ceased due to lack of application.

A similar condition existed on the leases of land at Sutton and Wilmington, whereby the leaseholder was required to distribute twelve bushels of peas and three bushels of wheat, which in 1835 was still being done.

Still in existence are The Draper's almshouses, in Margate, which were opened in 1710, and the number has grown from nine to forty-eight over the years. The houses are let to both single people and couples at very low rent, with the stipulation that 'no busy-body, nor proud idle person, nor waster' should be allowed to rent one, as stipulated by the founder, Michael Yoakley.

BRITANNIA, LADY OF VIRTUE: A MAID OF KENT ON THE COINS IN OUR POCKETS

A little-known fact is that the image of Britannia, so familiar to us all, was based on a portrait of a woman who lived in Kent.

The image of Britannia on UK coinage was based on a painting of Frances Stewart, a young lady of the court of King Charles II, who resisted the temptation to become one of his mistresses before she eventually married and moved to Cobham, near Rochester.

Prior to her marriage, she had posed for an image as 'Queen of the Sea' to be used on commemorative coins in 1664, and this image later became the basis for the Britannia which appeared on our coins from 1672. Many subtle changes have taken place on the Royal Mint images, and she now appears only on the 50p coin, with a trident in place of the spear, to emphasise our maritime connections.

BROOKLAND FONT AND THE LABOURS OF THE MONTH: A MEDIEVAL CALENDAR

The church at Brookland is remarkable for many reasons, not least the bell tower that stands separate from the church. A peek inside the church reveals many more strange sights: the painting of the murder of Thomas à Becket, the uneven number of arches either side of the chancel, and the lead font, one of only three in the county, showing the signs of the zodiac and the Labours of the Months. The depiction of both these sets of symbols is not unique in Britain, but Brookland is the only place they appear together.

The font dates to the twelfth century, and is inscribed with the names of the month and the signs of the zodiac in old French. The depictions of the tasks to be completed each month could be considered as a reminder to illiterate farmers, but in reality they would be well aware of what was needed; the font must surely be purely for decorative purposes. In January and February, the men depicted on the font celebrate the New Year and keep warm by the fire. When March arrives, they prune the vines and propagate in April. May is a time for hawking, either for pleasure or to keep birds from the crops, and in June and July they scythe and rake the hay. August and September are the times for reaping and threshing corn and in October, the wine grapes are pressed. November is the month for fattening the pig, ready for slaughtering in December.

The font is both beautiful and a reminder of our close relationship with the land. Kentish man was rarely idle (except possibly during the long winters, when it was prudent to stay indoors). Perhaps it was during these hours that the beautiful and surprising images around the Brookland font were created.

CANTERBURY MARBLES AND NINE MEN'S MORRIS: ANCIENT GAMES OF SKILL

The Canterbury marble is a clay marble, costing a penny or less, and was used in a specifically Kentish game of marbles. Larger than most marbles, measuring about 4cm across, the players had to flick a marble into one of a series of three depressions in the ground.

Another game that fascinated our ancestors was Nine Men's Morris, a more complicated version of Noughts and Crosses. The game was so popular in medieval times that workers on Canterbury Cathedral scratched boards into the bottom of the cloister seats so they could play in their breaks, where they can still be seen to this day.

CAPTAIN SWING: THE MAN THAT NEVER WAS

The economic depression following the Napoleonic Wars was exacerbated by bad harvests. The deprivation was felt keenly in rural Kent, and an unknown hand incited riots across the county.

Captain Swing first appeared in the 1830s in Lower Hardres, just outside Canterbury, burning hay ricks and smashing machines, and he made his presence known by sending letters to farmers, signed 'Captain Swing'. These were short, and often badly spelt, but were nonetheless threatening. The rioting spread throughout the Elham Valley and further afield to Dover and by the third week, over 100 machines had been destroyed.

The strangest thing about Captain Swing is that he never existed – he was a representation of the soul of the working man, a combination of every labourer who could not feed his family on his pitiful wages, or who had been replaced by an agricultural machine. The men who followed him paid a price, and hundreds were imprisoned, transported or even hanged.

The riots eventually died down and Captain Swing slipped quietly away.

CASTLES: THE HIGHEST NUMBER IN THE COUNTRY

Kent has more castles than any other county in the UK, due not only to its position as 'The Gateway to England', but also to its proximity to London: many of the great and the good who built castles needed relatively quick access to the capital.

There are thirty castles to be found in Kent, which come in all shapes and sizes, from Dover to Hever and Leeds to Chiddingstone through to the smaller ones like Walmer, Tonbridge and Saltwood. The grey ramparts of Rochester Castle loom above the town, while the creamy walls of Leeds Castle are reflected in the stillness of the moat around it, and all that remains of Eynesford Castle is the curtain wall.

Although built for defence, or to show power and privilege, none are now used in the defence of the realm, and many, like Lullingstone and Chilham, have been updated so often that they have crossed the line from castle to stately home, although they retain their name.

However, many were pressed into service once more during subsequent wars. Henry VIII's Walmer Castle is still the official home of the Warden of the Cinque Ports and was used by Wellington during the Napoleonic Wars. Dover Castle, built by the Normans, housed troops, was a command centre, and sheltered civilians from bomb attacks during the Second World War.

Cooling Castle.

Rochester Castle.

Many of our castles host re-enactment days, but on a quiet walk through a deserted bedroom or in the chill of an underground dungeon, visitors can sometimes hear the chink of armour or the ring of cobbled boots on stone floors.

A CAT SENT FROM GOD: HIS FELINE FRIEND WAS NOT FORGOTTEN

Sir Henry Wyatt of Allington Castle, located just to the north of Maidstone, was a regular at court, but was known as an outspoken adversary of Richard, Duke of Gloucester, which came to be his undoing. When Richard became King Richard II, having conveniently disposed of his nephews, Sir Henry was also locked in the Tower of London.

Left alone without food or warmth, it seemed that he was unlikely to survive – that is until the prison cat befriended him, bringing him birds to eat and sleeping with him at night. When Richard was defeated at the Battle of Bosworth Field, Henry was released, and although he did not stay in London, he never forgot the cat.

The family memorial in Boxley church, near Maidstone, includes a note on Sir Henry, saying 'God sent him a cat to feed and warm him.' The legend has persisted, and been embellished to include further details such as the fact that the jailer dressed the pigeons brought to the cell by the cat before serving them. Whatever the truth, cats are always welcome at Allington.

THE CATHEDRAL OF THE MARSH: KENT'S THIRD CATHEDRAL

The fact that Kent has two cathedrals, one at Rochester and one at Canterbury, is a well-known fact, but the people of Romney Marsh, that windswept southern wilderness, have dubbed St George's at Ivychurch 'The Cathedral of the Marsh'. It is one of our oldest churches, dating from at least the thirteenth century, although the many updates and restorations have all but obliterated the evidence.

The church is built of grey Kentish ragstone and creamy Caen stone, like Canterbury Cathedral, and has other similarities. The clerestory windows are the same as those in Canterbury, and now the box pews have been removed, the open space is reminiscent of the medieval ways of worship.

The village of Ivychurch is tiny, with less than 300 residents, so it is confusing to see such a large and impressive parish church. The land was once owned by the Bishops attached to Canterbury Cathedral, so it could have been a show of wealth and power. Or perhaps someone thought the local people deserved a taste of the glorious architecture that could be seen in the larger towns. The answer is lost in time.

The Cathedral of the Marsh, Romney Marsh.

THE CHATHAM CHEST: THE WORLD'S FIRST OCCUPATIONAL PENSION SCHEME

The Chatham Chest was a fund set up by Sir Francis Drake and Sir John Hawkins for the relief of seamen who were injured while in the service of Queen Elizabeth I, and thereafter unable to work. Each man gave a fixed sum from his wages, which was used for the relief of such as needed it.

The money was given out after an examination by the ship's physician, and was called Smart Money, awarded on a sliding scale, according to the type of injury. The injured man was required to obtain a Smart Ticket from the surgeon, which was countersigned by his captain, before being presented to the committee.

Sadly, the fund foundered because the amount deducted from each man's pay was a fixed amount and did not rise with inflation, so over time became insufficient to cover the payments required. It was eventually closed and the insurances were administered from Greenwich instead.

CHEESE PORTSMOUTH, ANYONE?: HOW THE NAME OF OUR FAVOURITE SNACK COULD HAVE BEEN VERY DIFFERENT

One hundred years before John Montague came up with the idea of making a sandwich so he could snack at the gaming table, his great-grandfather Sir Edward Montague was offered an earldom. Two titles were available: the Earl of Sandwich or the Earl of Portsmouth. He chose the Earl of Sandwich, as the town of Sandwich was at that time a port of huge national significance. This one small decision meant that the cheese and pickle portsmouth became the foodstuff that never was.

'CHERRY' INGRAM: CHERRY BLOSSOMS FROM BENENDEN RESTORE JAPAN'S HERITAGE

Until he was 40, Collingwood Ingram had never thought of being a horticulturalist. He loved the natural world, but his passion was birds, a field in which he excelled. However, when he moved to Benenden after the First World War, the flowering cherry trees in the garden captured his imagination, and within six years he was an expert on the subject.

Although he continued with his ornithological work, he soon became known as 'Cherry' Ingram, and as his collection grew, he travelled to Japan to see the trees in their native country.

Once in Japan, Ingram was saddened to hear that the trees were in decline. He suggested that new trees were grafted onto sturdy, wild trees to preserve their vigour, and was also able to reintroduce varieties of tree that were thought to be extinct, in particular the Akatsuke. Ingram had admired the particularly large blossoms in a friend's garden and had propagated his own, naming the tree Tai Haku, The Great White Cherry. Realising that the tree was a rarity, he sent cuttings to growers in Japan, where they flourished, and every one of the thousands of trees now growing around the world came from this one specimen.

THE CHERRYSTONE MURDER: KILLED FOR SCRUMPING CHERRIES

James Darling was only 10 years old when he was murdered by an irate farmer, who, it seems, found him scrumping cherries.

The only account we have is that on his grave, so without witnesses to tell us otherwise, it could have been a more organised crime, with James becoming the scapegoat. His grave is in Plumstead churchyard, and the inscription records the incident in detail. He died in July 1812, when Plumstead was still part of Kent, although it is now recognised as part of Greater London. The spelling in the poem below is as it appears on the gravestone:

Weep not for me my parents deer
There is no witness wanted here
The hammer of death was give to me
For eating cherries off the tree
Next morning death was to me so sweet
My blised Jesus for to meet
He did ease me of my pain
And I did join his holy train
The cruil one his death can't shun
For he most go when his glass is run
The horrows of death is sure to meet
And take his trail at the judgement seat

CHINESE, CANADIAN AND BELGIAN GRAVES AT SHORNCLIFFE: LEST WE FORGET

It is a surprise to see Chinese lettering on graves in Shorncliffe cemetery, but further investigation reveals that these are not the only nationals from across the globe buried nearby.

As the First World War ground on, the British government boosted forces by recruiting 100,000 Chinese from Wei Hai Wei, a small British territory on the Shandong Peninsula. The men served in France, and worked in Labour Corps away from the front line, and most returned to China as soon as the war ended. Six of those who died during their time in Europe are buried in the military cemetery at Shorncliffe.

The cemetery also holds the graves of many Canadian soldiers who were trained there. Some 40,000 Canadians were in the area in 1915, engaged in various training exercises, billeted in and around Hythe. From 1917 until the outbreak of the Second World War, the school children of Hythe travelled to Shorncliffe for Canadian Flower Day each June, which was organised to honour the dead of the Canadian regiments, of whom they had become fond.

The graveyard also contains a memorial to eighteen Belgian soldiers who lost their lives in defence of a free world.

THE CINQUE PORTS AND THEIR LIMBS: PROTECTING THE COUNTY FOR 1,000 YEARS

Created in the eleventh century by Edward the Confessor, the original members of the Cinque Port Confederation were Hastings, in East Sussex, along with Hythe, Romney, Dover and Sandwich in Kent.

Locals will know that by some vagary of the English language, or by corruption over time, the word 'cinque' has been anglicised and is pronounced 'sink'.

Fishergate, Sandwich.

These ports were required to provide ships ready to defend the country in times of need, with a certain number of men and boys, and the associated weaponry. In return, they were allowed relief on taxes owed to the Crown and were granted some measure of self-government, one example of this being the right of the ports to run their own courts.

The towns were overseen by the Admiralty Court, which was called into session as needed. The token of office used by the presiding judge was a mace shaped like an oar or tiller. The Latin word for a tiller is *gubernaculum*, and it is interesting to note that the word for the State Governor elections in the USA still in use today is 'gubernatorial'. Perhaps this comes solely from the derivation of the word 'governor', but it is tempting to think that it was taken to the New World from the ancient courts of Kent.

Other towns were later joined to the Confederation in a hierarchical structure, each becoming a 'limb' of one of the existing ports. Tenterden in Kent became a limb of Rye, Sussex. Lydd became a limb of New Romney, along with four smaller towns. Hythe was joined by West Hythe, and Deal and Ramsgate joined Sandwich, along with eight smaller villages. Lastly, Folkestone, Faversham and Margate became the limbs of Dover, with seven other villages. (*See* also 'Ship Money'.)

The Lord Warden of the Cinque Ports was once in control of the ports and the post-holder was known as The Keeper of the Coast. It is now an honorary title that is usually given to a member of the royal family or to a Prime Minister (the Duke of Wellington and the late Queen Mother are two notable examples).

COAL POSTS AND A COAL RUSH: WAYSIDE MARKERS FOR THE COAL AGE

You may see a white cast-iron post on your way from Kent to London and wonder what they are. They are, in fact, coal posts.

A ring of these Coal Tax Posts was erected at a distance of 20 miles around London in 1861 to replace the previous posts that had been put up after the Great Fire of London in 1666. The posts worked in much the same way as the signs warning motorists of the Congestion Charge, reminding businessmen that coal coming into London was subject to taxation, initially at a rate of 4*d* a ton. Many of the posts can still be seen by the roadside and on verges, including seventeen in Swanley and Crockenhill, and an equal number in Bromley, which many residents still consider to be part of Kent, although it has now officially been subsumed into Greater London. Most of the posts are now Grade II listed monuments.

The coal rush of east Kent happened almost a hundred years later, when the ship *Aqueity* ran aground on the Nayland Rocks with a full cargo of coal. The date was 24 December 1938, and for the people of Margate, Christmas certainly did come early that year. Almost 200 tons of coal was jettisoned from the ship before she was pulled off the rocks, and during that time, men, women and children climbed, waded and paddled over the rocks and into the water to retrieve the precious cargo. *Pathe News* footage shows whole families using any bucket, basket or bag they could find to salvage as much of the bounty as possible – a short-lived but welcome treat in the depths of winter.

CONCRETE RADAR: CUTTING-EDGE TECH FROM THE FIRST WORLD WAR

Both the First and Second World Wars led to great strides in the fields of technology and medicine, but perhaps none is as weird as the huge concrete structures installed on the south coast to warn of the advance of the enemy.

The first 'sound mirror' was installed on the south coast of Kent during the First World War, and was a 15ft concave concrete dish, in front of which stood the listener with a trumpet-shaped 'sound collector'.

Concrete radars at Denge, near Dungeness.

The site at Fan Bay continued to be used for experiments in this field, and more mirrors were added at Joss Gap, the Isle of Sheppey, Lade, Abbot's Cliff and West Hythe. These new sound mirrors were 20ft in diameter, and at this stage, the listener still had to stand in front of the device. Working together, the mirrors at Abbot's Cliff, West Hythe and Lade allowed listeners to triangulate the position of approaching aircraft.

As they developed, the mirrors increased in size, and it was deemed sensible for a control room to be built underneath them. Lade was also the site of a 200ft-long concrete wall, standing 26ft high, which was a 'wall mirror' and operated in the same way as the circular devices. The sound mirrors were surprisingly effective, but due to increases in aircraft technology, were abandoned in 1939. Other such structures were built in other parts of the country, but Lade is the only place where visitors can see all three types still standing.

COUNT ZBOROWSKI: INVENTOR OF A FAMOUS RAILWAY AND A FAMOUS CAR

Count Louis Zborowski lived fast and died young, but has left an indelible mark on the Kent landscape and in the hearts of cinema-goers across the world.

It was Zborowski, with his friend Captain J.E.P. Howey, who conceived and built the Romney Hythe & Dymchurch Light Railway, creating the one-third scale engines and laying the track. Sadly, Zborowski was killed before the track was finished, but his name is forever linked with it.

The Count's other claim to fame is that he designed the racing car that was immortalised by Ian Fleming as Chitty Chitty Bang Bang. The car he named Chitty Bang Bang and his subsequent racing cars were built in Canterbury while he lived at Higham Park, just outside the town in the village of Bridge.

THE COUNTLESS STONES: TRY TO COUNT THEM IF YOU DARE

The so-called Countless Stones are part of the Medway Megaliths – ancient stones sited around the River Medway, and are part of the Kit's Coty House monument. Known variously as the Lower Kit's Coty House or Little Kit's Coty House stones, they are more usually referred to as the Countless Stones.

The stones are so old that their origins are unknown, and many stories have grown up around them over time.

Of little importance in themselves, they form part of the larger pattern of stone monuments in the area, and have drawn their fair share of folklore and legend. The exact number of stones has always been in question, hence the name, and it is said that they are impossible to count. A baker once attempted a count, by placing a bread roll on stones he had already counted, but the Devil moved them, ate them, or disguised himself as an extra roll. There are at least three endings to the story, but it is generally agreed that the poor man either lost his mind or just dropped dead from exhaustion.

CRICKET: THE COUNTRY'S NATIONAL SPORT BEGAN IN KENT

Long known as the birthplace of cricket and home to the prestigious Kent County Cricket Club, who play in Canterbury, Kent is not only the birthplace of Colin Cowdrey, Frank Woolley, Les Ames and Alan Knott, but also of John Willes, who introduced round-arm bowling.

Until the move was introduced by Willes in the early nineteenth century, cricket balls were bowled underarm. Legend has it that while practising in the family barn, with his dog as outfielder, he drafted in his sister to bowl so he could practise his swing. Hampered by the wide skirts of the time, she threw the ball round-arm, which her brother quickly adopted and introduced to his teammates. Although still part of the game rules, unlike underarm bowling, modern bowlers now favour over-arm bowling.

The St Lawrence Ground, now known less romantically as The Spitfire Ground, was once the site of the St Lawrence Leper Hospital, and featured that most unusual of sights – a tree on the pitch. The old lime tree had been played around for so long that it became part of local tradition and was used in play until high winds of 2005 finally killed it, 158 years after it was planted.

Another more dangerous tradition is the practice of playing a game of cricket on the Goodwin Sands. The Sands are well-known amongst sailors for the centuries of shipwrecks that have occurred there, and the area has gained notoriety as 'Calamity Corner'. The first cricket match recorded on the Sands was in 1824, organised by Ramsgate harbourmaster Captain K. Martin, but charity matches are still played there even today. Players arrive at the Sands by boat just before low tide and wait for the first moment they can step onto dry(ish) land. They then have less than an hour to play before returning to the mainland.

CURFEW BELLS: STILL RINGING OUT ACROSS THE COUNTY

Curfew bells were first introduced by King William I and were the signal for everyone to put out their fires before they went to bed, named after the French *couvre feu* or fire cover, and were a legal requirement in every town and village throughout England. It was, in effect, a measure to ensure public safety, as one house fire could affect a whole street.

Kent is a county that likes its traditions and clings to them jealously. Only a handful of towns now have a curfew bell that sounds regularly, but the inhabitants are understandably proud of this link with the past.

Henry Edwards tells us in his book *A Collection of Old English Customs* of 1842 that the curfew bell of St Margaret's at Cliffe, between Dover and Deal, is paid for by the proceeds of an ancient charitable trust, set up in 1696. Five rods of land were put into trust by a shepherd who had fallen over the cliff, which paid for the curfew bell between September and April. A similar charity was set up in Ringwould, to allow the bell to ring daily between 2 November and 2 February.

Two towns that proudly keep up the tradition of ringing a curfew bell are the ancient port of Sandwich and the cathedral city of Canterbury, although the Bell Harry bell at Canterbury is now sounded electronically.

The bell at Sandwich was once known as the pig bell, telling inhabitants that they could allow their pigs out to graze, and it was sister to an early morning bell known as the goose bell, which reminded them to get the pigs in and put out the geese for the day. Despite some resistance, the bells continue to this day.

THE DADD MURDER: COMMON CRIMINAL OR TORTURED GENIUS?

The paintings of Richard Dadd are surprisingly collectable, considering his criminal past. He was born in Chatham in 1817 and after a promising start, began to show signs of mental illness whilst on an expedition with Sir Thomas Phillips to the Middle East. Dadd had already gained a reputation as an artist and in 1842 he was asked to accompany Sir Thomas to record the trip, as these were the days before photography.

On his return to England in 1843, Richard went home, but was plagued with thoughts that the Devil was directing his actions. An eminent physician recommended that he be confined to a mental institution, but his father was reluctant to do this, and instead took Richard for a short break to Cobham, where they booked rooms in a pub.

Later that day, Richard stabbed his father to death in Cobham Park and left him in a shallow grave in an area now known colourfully as Dadd's Hole, leaving money, gold watch and silver spectacles on the body. It was this that tipped off the police that the crime was murder, not robbery.

A notice was printed for circulation, giving details of Richard's appearance. He was described as having 'dark hair, a scar on the forehead, light blue eyes, heavy dark eyebrows' and wearing a dark coat and sky-blue trousers; he was only 21 years old. The leaflet went on to say that 'his manner is reserved and sullen, he has a hurried gait and the appearance incident to persons labouring under a loss of intellect', though who gave this description is not known. A reward of £10 was offered for information that led to his capture.

Richard was eventually caught and admitted to Bethlem Hospital's Criminal Lunatic Department (commonly known as Bedlam) in 1844, where he remained for the next twenty years. He was then moved to Broadmoor, where he died in 1886 from lung disease.

He continued to paint throughout his life and his paintings are now highly sought after, even appearing in the catalogue of the Tate Gallery. They show fantastic scenes of fairies and other supernatural beings, illustrated in minute detail by the artist, along with disturbing depictions of patients suffering from mental illness.

The site of the murder is said to be haunted, and repeated attempts to fill in the depression have been unsuccessful, as the ground simply drops again after new earth is added. Dadd and his paintings continue to evoke mixed feelings, from those who wish to see a reflection of a damaged mind to those who contest that his artistic genius was only slightly dampened by his disability.

DADDLUMS OR KENTISH SKITTLES: A PUB GAME THAT'S ENJOYING A REVIVAL

Daddlums is a peculiarly Kentish form of skittles once played in pubs and bars throughout the county. Today, only a handful of places keep a board, and these are rapidly disappearing; one of the few is The Jolly Drayman in Gravesend.

The game is played on a rectangular table just over 5ft long and about 2ft wide. It is set up at about knee height, supported underneath on trestles for stability. The board is surrounded on three sides by wooden shuttering. Nine small pins, measuring just 3in high, are set up in a diamond pattern on the table and players take turns to throw three wooden 'cheeses' from a distance of 9ft away, no mean feat after a few pints, as the cheeses are small enough to fit comfortably into a man's hand.

This game might be the one that is often referred to in historical documents as 'cales' or 'keals', a particularly Kentish version of nine-pin skittles.

A daddlums table.

DEADMAN'S ISLAND: SETTING FREE THE BONES OF THE PAST

More than 200 years after they were buried, the bones of long-dead prisoners are beginning to resurface along the north coast of Kent. During the early nineteenth century, prisoners were held on decommissioned ships moored just offshore, once used as quarantine ships. The ships were known as 'prison hulks' and the men who died, especially those who succumbed to contagious diseases, were buried on the uninhabited Deadman's Island, just off the Isle of Sheppey, 6ft deep but in plain unmarked coffins.

Constant tidal erosion and rising sea levels have now combined to lift the coffins, and wooden slats are mixed with bones on the surface of the mudflats. As the island is a designated Site of Special Scientific Interest, it is not accessible to the public, and as the bones are being taken by the sea as they loosen, it is unlikely that they will ever be collected and re-interred.

THE DEAF ADDER OF SEVENOAKS: HIS DEAFNESS COULD SAVE YOU

There is an old tale that tells of a deaf adder that lived in the woods near Sevenoaks. It could not hear, but if it caught sight of you, it would follow you wherever you went, no matter how far away, and its bite was always fatal.

Scary as this seems, the most unusual part of the tale is that the markings on the back of the snake seemed to read;

If I could hear as well as I can see
Nobody should escape from me.

This report was taken from the 1860s, but I have no reason to doubt that the descendants of this animal still live in the woods, and are still on the lookout for unwary travellers.

DENEHOLES: A MEDIEVAL FARMING PRACTICE

Deneholes are a feature of chalky landscapes, and appear in the south of England, mainly in Kent and Essex. But what are they?

Ranging between 10 and 70 metres deep, these shafts, which seem to be randomly placed in the landscape, end not in a single cave, but in a daisy-like array of several caverns. For years they perplexed historians, who linked them with the Romans or the Danes. In actual fact, they could be of any date from the Middle Ages onwards, and their purpose was not for the disposal of bodies or the control of prisoners – they were chalk mines. The lower level of chalk contained minerals beneficial to the depleted topsoil, and was dug up and spread upon the fields by local farmers. When spent, the holes were filled in with loose rubble, which settled over the years, giving an indication of their position.

THE DEVIL'S IN THE DETAIL: THE DEVIL IS EVERYWHERE

The Devil's Stone

A curious stone stands at the entrance to the grounds of Newington church, known as the Devil's Stone. The stone was moved from its original position in Church Lane when its sister stone was broken up and used as part of a wall, and it now stands alone.

The outline of a footprint can be seen on the front of the stone, and local folk tales tell us that the mark is the footprint of the devil, made when he jumped from the church tower carrying the bells that he had stolen.

The stone is said to spark when hit with a pebble, and to bring good luck to children who place one finger on top of the stone and walk round it three times.

The Devil's Kneading Trough

The Devil is also referenced in the name of one of the most spectacular sights on the North Downs. The Devil's Kneading Trough is a steep-sided valley and as it was not cut from the chalk by the passage of a river, it seems to be an anomaly. Unable to explain its presence, locals presumed it had supernatural origins and gave it the unusual name, which quickly led to its reputation as a place of intrigue; anyone who walks the boundaries seven times and drinks from the spring will be sure to meet the Devil himself.

This area of Wye is now a protected area, but some of the older local residents may remember hearing about the Easter Monday of 1928 when the Ashford

Grass Track Speedway Club arrived in the valley. Some 3,000 spectators gathered to watch the bravest of the club attempt the 400-yard track to the summit. 'Sonny' Hanson, on his Velocette 347cc bike claimed victory, riding up the one-in-three gradient course in just over 23 seconds.

The Devil's Den

There is a significant medieval moated site at Edenbridge, which is now called The Devil's Den. The origins of the name have been lost in the mists of time, but something mysterious must have happened here for the name to be buried so deeply in local folklore.

The Devil's Drop

Sharpness Cliff in Dover was once known as The Devil's Drop. This was because it was used in the execution of prisoners in medieval times. A quick shove in the small of the back and the deed was done. Interestingly, the old Roman Pharos lighthouse had a similar name: The Devil's Drop of Mortar.

The Devil and St Dunstan

Lastly, one of the most well-known instances of the Devil in Kent is his appearance to St Dunstan in Tunbridge Wells. The Devil, disguised as a young woman, appeared to St Dunstan while he was working at his forge. St Dunstan was not fooled and grabbed the Devil by the nose with his red-hot tongs. The Devil cooled his burning nose in the waters of the well, which have ever since been tinged with a distinctly iron-rich taste.

DIAMONDS AT BEARSTED: PRECIOUS GEMS FROM THE HILLSIDE

A report of 1834 describes the semi-precious stones that became known as Bearsted Diamonds. They were small crystals found in the sand deposits and were mined, cut and polished to be used in jewellery.

These were possibly selenite crystals, of the type that can still be found in the London clay around the Thames Estuary, but who knows: it might still be possible to find a diamond in the Kentish soil.

DICK AND SAL AT CANTERBURY FAIR: LOCAL DIALECT IS OUR HERITAGE

William Caxton was born in the Weald of Kent, and travelled to Europe to learn skills in the new art of printing, which he brought back to the UK. In the preface to one of his early works, he says he 'was born and lemed myne English in Kente in the Weeld, where English is spoken broad and rude.'

One of the fascinating facts about the standardisation of the English language through the medium of print is that the editor had a great deal of control over the language in his books. Caxton himself wrote a story to illustrate the confusion that can arise when people from different ends of the country use distinctive dialect words.

Dick and Sal at Canterbury Fair is one of the few works of literature written in the Kentish dialect, which makes it linguistically important, although it is only a simple doggerel poem.

The poem was written in 1822 by John White Masters. Dick and Sal travel from Sheldwich, through Perry Wood, along Shanford (the dialect pronunciation of Shalmsford) Street, up to the Chartham Downs and into Canterbury at Wincheap, which was the main route into Canterbury before the A28 was built. After several adventures, they returned home by the same route.

Dick and Sal at Canterbury Fair may not be as famous as works such as Chaucer's *The Canterbury Tales*, but it is an honest poem, reflecting the lives of ordinary, working people, and is a charming reflection of the era.

Bessie Marchant is another author who wrote in the Kentish dialect, using it in her first three books, including one that dealt with the Marion Persecutions. After this, she either chose or was coerced to write in standard English, and became a pioneer in the genre of girls' adventure fiction.

DISPUTED DOG OWNERSHIP: A FARCICAL CASE LEAVES THE JUDGE BEMUSED

An unusual and somewhat farcical court case was reported in the *Folkestone Observer* in November 1864 concerning the ownership of a lurcher. Richard Baker and John Richardson both contested that they were the rightful owner, and brought witnesses to support their case.

The case report is surprisingly detailed, going backwards and forwards between the two parties. John Richards said he had bought the dog, Ben, for

4*s* and a glass of beer, from a man who had himself bought the dog to work his sheep but found it to be unsuitable.

Richard Baker said that the dog was his, and asserted that he had paid a sovereign for it, plus a donkey. He had left the dog in Folkestone several weeks earlier but had got drunk in Romney Fair and been locked up, so he had been unable to go back for it.

Each man brought witnesses to attest to the purchase and subsequent ownership, but after many statements the judge dismissed the case without judgement. Perhaps he felt it was a waste of court time, or perhaps he just found it impossible to make a decision. Sadly, we will never know who finally kept the dog.

A DOG COLLAR MUSEUM: THE ONLY ONE IN THE WORLD

The Dog Collar Museum, housed in the grounds of Leeds Castle, is surely one of the greatest eccentricities of the people of Kent. The museum has 130 dog collars, ranging in age from medieval collars to those used in Victorian times. The museum is surprisingly intriguing and welcomes half a million visitors a year.

The original collection was presented to the castle in the 1970s and since then has continued to grow, by acquisition and by public donation. It now includes collars from all over the world and shows examples once worn by tiny pampered pooches as well as those worn by guard dogs ten times their size.

DOG WHIPPER'S LAND: ORDER IN CHURCH!

Henry Edwards (*see* Curfew Bells) describes a charge of 10*s* as rent on 2 acres of land in Chislet knowns as Dog Whipper's Marsh. This money was paid to the owner of the land, Sir John Bridges, who used the money to pay for a man to keep order during divine service in church.

In actual fact, the post of Dog Whipper was a common one up until the nineteenth century. The post-holder was issued with a long stick or whip along with a pair of wooden 'dog tongs' and was responsible for taking control of any dogs in and around the church, particularly during service. This mostly entailed the control of stray dogs, but could also include separating any domestic dogs that had followed their master into the church and seen the opportunity for a fight when they got bored.

The work was carried out as part of other duties at the church of All Saints in Eastchurch. In 1672 the clerk received 10*s* as six months' pay for whipping the dogs and in 1676 the beadle was paid 1*s*, for keeping dogs out of the church.

There is also evidence for a Dog Whipper being employed in Birchington, from as early as 1622. The use of the land known as Dog Acre was allowed as 'payment in kind' to the post-holder, who could farm the land or rent it out as he pleased. To the modern eye, this may seem a large payment for a small service, but in the days before rabies had been brought under control, the job of a Dog Whipper would have been a dangerous one, as a bite from a rabid dog could lead to a slow and painful death. There is now only a small part of the Birchington Dog Acre left undeveloped, opposite The Seaview public house.

DR SYN AND THE SCARLET PIMPERNEL: CHARACTERS FROM THE FIFTH CONTINENT

It will come as no surprise that the dark and mysterious landscape of the Romney Marsh has given rise to not one but two swashbuckling heroes.

Romney Marsh.

The errant vicar Dr Christopher Syn was created in 1915 by Russell Thorndike and was the hero of seven adventures. Dr Syn was a model clergyman by day, but at night he took the code name Cap'n Clegg (alias The Scarecrow) and became a dashing smuggler, outwitting the Riding Officers and helping the poor. The character became so popular that he has now appeared in several films and is celebrated regularly in the town of Dymchurch, on the Romney Marshes, in the bi-annual Day of Syn celebrations.

Every other August, Dr Syn comes to life as The Scarecrow, along with as many smugglers, Dragoons, pirates, press-gangs and highwayman as can be mustered. They wreak havoc, carousing on the beaches, staging mock-battles, and parading through the town accompanied by musicians and Morris dancers.

The Scarlet Pimpernel was created in Kent by Baroness Emmuska Orczy and her husband Montague Barstow in 1903. Sir Percy Blakeney lived in Kent and probably left for the continent from Romney Marsh, where the scarlet pimpernel plant grows. Transforming into his alter-ego the Scarlet Pimpernel, Blakeney brought many a French refugee across the English Channel at the time of the French Revolution, using the same routes the smugglers had travelled many years before.

DUDLEY DIGGES AND THE RUNNING FIELD: SIR DUDLEY AND THE RACES OF OLD WIVES LEES

In 1639, Sir Dudley Digges, MP for the area and owner of Chilham Castle, left money in his will for two young men and two maidens between the ages of 16 and 24 to win in a running race held in May each year. One man and one woman could win £10 each, a not inconsiderable sum in those days. What young person could resist the chance to show off their sporting prowess and have a chance of such riches at the same time?

The race was held at Old Wives Lees, near Chilham, at a place that was called the Running Field. The event proved to be so popular that the scheme was extended to include a second race at Sheldwich, near Faversham, where there was a similarly named field.

The races continued until 1850, when the high moral standards of Victorian society censured it as an unseemly activity. The scanty attire of the runners and the rowdy behaviour of the crowds caused concern amongst the administrators, who decided to donate the money to the school instead of to the winners of a race.

THE DUMB BORSHOLDER OF CHART: NOT AS DUMB AS IT SOUNDS

The Dumb Borsholder of Chart is a wooden staff measuring just over a metre in length with only one of its four iron rings remaining, and a sharpened length of iron attached to one end, giving it the appearance of a weapon. Historians cannot agree on its age, its use, or even how it came to be in Wateringbury.

The small village of Chart was located near Wateringbury, but is now one of the lost villages of Kent. Perhaps it was gradually abandoned due to lack of employment in the area, or perhaps the village was purposely sacked and razed to the ground. Another theory is that the village was burnt to stop the spread of the plague.

Whatever the reason for its decline, historical artefacts rescued from the village are now held in Wateringbury, the most interesting of which is the Dumb Borsholder of Chart.

This mysterious object could be a remnant of Anglo-Saxon occupation, a baton for a constable, or even a purely ceremonial item. Perhaps we will never know its true use, although we do know that the word 'bossalder' may have derived from the Middle English language meaning 'senior person of the village' and denoted the person who collected the village tithes. Pegge's *Alphabet of Kenticisms* tells us that the old Kentish word for tither was 'borow'.

The Dumb Borsholder was carried by an elected representative of the village to the annual meetings of the local Hundred (*see* Lathes) in Yalding, and it was used as a sign of authority to speak on behalf of the village even though no elder was officially appointed. The tiny hamlet consisted of only twelve houses, and each tenant took turns to carry the Dumb Borsholder each year, taking with him the tax of one penny per household.

The Dumb Borsholder of Chart, now in Wateringbury church.

EDENBRIDGE'S BONFIRE OF TRAITORS: THREE TRAITORS GET THEIR JUST DESERTS

For almost 100 years, the town of Edenbridge, located on the Kent/Surrey border near Sevenoaks, has hosted a bonfire celebration on the Saturday nearest to 5 November, similar to the more well-known parades in Sussex. The parade of floats and costumed revellers is led by a Gunpowder Bishop and the peculiarly Kentish twist to this event is that the effigies of three traitors are burnt: Guy Fawkes, General Wolfe and Anne Boleyn.

ELEPHANTS IN THE GROUNDS: DID THEY LANDSCAPE THE GARDENS?

Elephants were supposedly brought to Chilham Castle to clear the newly redesigned grounds, but the Chilham Castle website is circumspect on the matter and says that contemporary documentation can neither prove nor disprove this story. It would be lovely to find out that it was true. A building on the edge of castle property considered to be The Elephant House is still visible from the main road, so perhaps it is.

ELHAM MURDERS: BLOOD DRIPPED THROUGH THE CEILING

The quiet village of Elham is known today as a place of calm and tranquillity. On the morning of 30 September 1846, however, the whole hamlet was buzzing after the dreadful discovery of the dead body of 31-year-old Sharruck Rudd Bragg and his barely alive family.

The gruesome scene was discovered by the couple's lodger, who gave witness that there was so much blood that it had dripped through the floor into the ceiling of the room below. Upon noticing the blood, his immediate reaction was to call a neighbour and send her upstairs to investigate.

It appeared that Bragg had badly beaten his wife and 3-year-old daughter with a hammer before cutting his own throat. By mid-morning the next day, both wife and child were also dead. Amazingly, not all the family perished in this miserable tale. Nestled close to the body of her mother, four-month-old Mary had miraculously survived, and was taken from the scene by her aunt.

A short inquest was carried out at the local public house, and a verdict was returned that Bragg had carried out the murders and suicide while 'not in a sound state of mind', as evidenced by numerous accounts of his recent 'low moods'.

The funeral was well-attended and it seems that the whole family had been popular in the neighbourhood. Had Bragg had the feelings of paranoia ascribed to him in the twenty-first century, it is hoped that he would have received the help he needed and this tragedy would never have happened.

The cottage in which the murders took place still stands, and is known as Anne's Cottage, The Row, Elham.

ERLE-DRAX: THE MAD MAJOR

John Samuel Wanley Sawbridge lived at Olantigh Towers in the beautiful Wye Valley, now designated as an Area of Outstanding Natural Beauty, having married the heiress Jane Erle-Drax. Upon their marriage, he changed his name from Sawbridge to Erle-Drax, presumably because it had a more aristocratic ring to it, and they divided their time between Jane's property in Devon and Olantigh House, which he had inherited from his father. Known locally as the Mad Major, from his rank in the East Kent Volunteers, Erle-Drax was at one time MP for Wareham.

Before his death, Erle-Drax was keen to dictate every aspect of his funeral, and even arranged for a 'dry run' of the event, reports of which read like the script from a present-day black comedy, ending up with the dummy being taken from the coffin and flung into a nearby hedge.

The Mad Major was fond of art and statuary, and had a large private art collection in his home. He was the first owner of the Hubert Fountain, which eventually found is way to Victoria Park in Ashford (*see* Fountain Fun), and planned for a life-sized statue of himself to be erected, hoping for it to be shown in a prominent position in London. Sadly, his appeals for donations failed to raise enough money, so he paid for the statue himself, which showed him moustachioed and macho, mounted on a prancing horse and waving his top hat. The statue stood outside the entrance to Olantigh House for thirty years before it was removed by his nephew.

FANNY WALLACE: ACQUITTED ON GROUNDS OF INSANITY

The sad story of Fanny Wallace shows that Victorian judges and juries did show compassion in their verdicts, even though they may be represented in popular fiction as heartless and judgemental.

Unmarried Frances 'Fanny' Wallace worked as a laundress in Dover, and in 1851 bore an illegitimate daughter. Despite being highly strung and prone to bouts of hypochondria, she raised the child through the first five years of her life, and witnesses attest that she doted on the girl, who was also called Fanny.

Having kept the details of the child's parentage a secret for many years, she at last came to trust someone enough to divulge her secret, and in 1856 revealed that the father had in fact been her brother-in-law. Suddenly hysterical at the thought that her sister might be told, she cut the throat of the child and ran into the street, shouting, 'I have been and murdered my own child!'

Fanny was convicted of murder at Dover and sent to Maidstone for sentencing. Luckily, the judge was moved by her story and by the many witness accounts of her love for her child, and her previous episodes of mental instability. Fanny was not executed, but remained locked up for the rest of her life, which, in retrospect, may indeed have been the punishment less easy to bear for a mother who had felt herself compelled to murder her own child.

FARNINGHAM HOME FOR LITTLE BOYS: GROUNDBREAKING CHILDCARE IN THE EIGHTEENTH CENTURY

The Farningham Home for Little Boys, situated near Horton Kirby, was a pioneering home for orphans and destitute boys that showed a level of care way beyond its time.

The horrors of Victorian orphanages were well documented by Charles Dickens and other writers of the time, and an alternative provision was long overdue. The home was founded in 1863 by three London philanthropists who wanted to offer something different from the austere institutions of the time, and the Farningham Home for Little Boys was born. The system gave each boy a home in a large house with a house-mother and house-father looking after thirty resident boys. The boys, thus cared for, were also educated and taught a trade, while living in the village complete with chapel, sports field and communal buildings. Ten homes were built on the site, including one where 'old boys' could stay when they visited.

The memories of boys who lived at the home show that their time there was, in the main, happy, although somewhat severe.

THE FATE OF THE REVENUE OFFICERS: LOST FOR 150 YEARS

The life of a Revenue Officer was hard. They were employed to stop the huge loss of taxes brought about by the practice of smuggling goods to and from the continent, which was rife in both Kent and nearby Sussex. Two kinds of men applied for the jobs: those intent on upholding the law and those who wished to benefit from regular payments to ensure they looked the other way when a smuggled shipment went past.

It will come as no surprise to learn that the life was a hard one, and that the officers were not well-liked by many of the local community, standing as they did as agents of the government. At the height of the smuggling era, two hard-working Revenue Officers from Hythe went to work one night and never came home to their families. Despite extensive searches, they were not found, but neither were their bodies. Their families grieved and time moved on.

One hundred and fifty years later, a builder undertaking renovation work on The Bell Inn, in Hythe, revealed their fate. Nobody was brought to justice, but it was clear that they had both been murdered, for their bodies, still in full uniform, had been bricked up behind the inglenook fireplace. The pub was an infamous smugglers' haunt, with secret passages, steps inside the huge chimney so it could be used as a lookout post and an exposed underground stream down which barrels could be floated. It seems that the men were murdered while doing their duty, and that their killers will never be known, although two ghosts have been seen at the pub, sitting by the fireplace. Perhaps, one day, they will reveal their fate and the identities of the murderers.

FLEMISH ARCHITECTURE: A LITTLE TASTE OF THE NETHERLANDS

East Kent, from Margate to Canterbury, is spattered with houses that typify the type of architecture we associate with the Netherlands of 300 or 400 years ago. Curly gables, decorative tie-bars, integral dates and crow-steps all give a flavour of the style which has become known as 'Dutch'. Concentrated in Sandwich, a port that had a large Dutch population, the easily identifiable style can be seen in Deal, Ash, Minster and Wingham, for example, appearing on tiny cottages as well as larger houses.

Flemish architecture in east Kent.

Until more detailed research is undertaken, we cannot say for certain why or for whom these houses were built, but we can agree that they are a beautiful and valued feature of the architecture of Kent.

FOLKESTONE BEEF: SOUNDS FISHY ...

Francis Buckland, writing about the *Curiosities of Natural History* in 1861, describes his surprise when, on a visit to Folkestone harbour, he noticed that almost all the houses were hung with lines of drying fish, strung out like bunting. On asking what type of fish it was, he was told it was 'Folkestone beef', which was a mixture of rig, huss, bull-huss, fiddler and other types of fish. By reference to an illustrated book of fish types, he learnt that the rig was a dogfish, the huss or robin huss was a small spotted dogfish, the bull-huss was a large spotted dogfish and the fiddler was an angel or shark ray.

The fish were prepared as soon as they were landed, having their heads, tails and fins removed before they were split in half, salted and hung up to dry. The heads and intestines were used for bait and the livers were boiled for oil.

This very curious cottage industry shows that fishing in Folkestone was not organised by one central company, but was carried out individually by each man and his family.

FOLKESTONE PIER: SITE OF THE VERY FIRST BEAUTY PAGEANT

Whatever your opinion of the world of beauty pageants, there is no denying that they have brought pleasure to a lot of people.

The very first international pageant was the brainchild of the Managing Director of Folkestone's Victoria Pier, Robert Forsyth. Today, there is nothing left of the pier, which was situated below the Cliff Lift, near Marine Parade, but in 1908 it was new and very much in vogue.

The pageant was created as a way of attracting visitors to the newly opened venue, and every modern competition can be traced back to this one event, which was the first competition to invite entrants from other countries to participate. The winner of that very first contest was Miss Nellie Jarman from London.

FOUNTAIN FUN: A SINGING FOUNTAIN FOR A BIRTHDAY TREAT

The Hubert Fountain in Ashford is a wonder to behold; its over-the-top design is a perfect representation of Victorian design, and it is now a listed monument. Made of cast iron, the fountain shows children from four continents of the world at the topmost level, nubile bare-breasted women and muscular men on the mid-section, and cherubs and water sprites on the lower level.

The Hubert Fountain, Victoria Park, Ashford.

The novel concept of including sixty-four whistles in the construction allowed the fountain to 'sing' as the water poured out past a water-driven organ mechanism. It is somewhat of a surprise, then, to find that it was not at first wanted by the worthies of Ashford Council.

The fountain was built in France in 1862 and shown in the Royal Horticultural Society's Gardens in London for the Second Great International Exhibition before it was bought by John Sawbridge Erle-Drax and moved to Olantigh Towers, a country house in Wye. After a fire at the house in 1903, the fountain was put up for sale and was bought in 1910 by George Harper, who wanted to donate the fountain to the people of Ashford. The council refused to pay the cost of removal, and declined Mr Harper's kind offer. Not to be put off, George offered to pay for the removal and re-erection of the fountain if the council paid for the foundations and a water supply that would ensure the fountain flowed at least once a year, on 23 July, his birthday.

The fountain was used to commemorate the coronation of Elizabeth II in 1953 and again on her Silver Jubilee in 1977, when it was refurbished. It underwent further refurbishment in 2007, but it was not possible to save the whistles and get them to play.

The fountain has now been named, somewhat condescendingly, as the Fountain of Delight.

FREDERICK ROBSON: A SUPERSTAR OF HIS AGE

Thomas Brownbill, born in Margate in 1821, never grew to more than 5ft tall, and yet he was a huge sensation on the London theatres under the name Frederick Robson.

Coming to the stage at a time when realism was only just creeping into the performances of the greatest actors, Robson brought a taste of authentic pathos to his roles, and quickly became a star, being asked to give performances for Queen Victoria on several occasions.

Robson had honed his craft in provincial theatre during his 20s, in particular spending time in Whitstable where he perfected the Kentish accent, which he used in many of his later roles.

His fame was widespread, as his tragi-comic characters tore at the heartstrings of his audience. The writer Westland Marston, writing in 1888, says that 'It was perhaps … his union of the terrible with the droll which most recommended him to general favour'.

Sadly, he was only to enjoy ten years of fame, and died at the age of 43, having retired from the stage some years earlier, due to illness.

A FRENCH CHAPEL IN CANTERBURY CATHEDRAL: REFUGEES WELCOMED BY THE CHURCH OF ENGLAND

The Black Prince's Chantry in Canterbury Cathedral was set up at the time of his marriage to Joan Holland in the mid-1360s. Joan was known as the Fair Maid of Kent, not because she lived here, but because her father was the Earl of Kent. Although Joan is not buried in Kent, her husband Edward rests in the cathedral, depicted on his tomb in full armour.

In 1575, when the town was filling with Walloon refugees fleeing religious persecution in Belgium, Elizabeth I gave them the privilege of using the chapel for services in their own language.

To avoid calling attention to themselves, the worshippers entered the chapel through a side door, which can still be seen today. Services in French are still held weekly by the *Eglise Protestante Française de Cantorbéry* (the French Protestant Church of Canterbury) at 3 p.m. each Sunday.

THE GARLANDS OF MAYTIME: A LOST TRADITION

May Day was also known as Garland Day, and there is much photographic evidence of the use of garlands during May Day celebrations across the county. In both Rochester and Sevenoaks, children paraded with decorated hoops and sticks, calling at houses to sing, in the same way that they did at Christmastime.

The *Maidstone Journal* of 1890 reported that the custom of garlanding was still carried out 'in many country places'. Two hoops were joined crosswise and decorated with flowers, ribbons, and occasionally a doll dressed in white and green. The pretty picture of girls walking sedately in pairs is somewhat marred, as we read that it was a tradition for boys to pick handfuls of nettles and try to whip the faces of 'any person they met'. I suspect that this treatment was reserved for other children and not for respected members of the community.

During the eighteenth century, the first of May was called Flowering Day in Tonbridge, and the task of decorating the town fell to the pupils of the Tonbridge School, which was at that time sponsored by The Skinners Company. When members of The Skinners Society visited, the town, church and school were decorated with flowers by the boys.

The crowning of a May Queen in villages across the area has recently been revived, but garlanding is one of the skills that has now been lost in the mists of time.

THE GATES OF THANET: THROUGH THE CLIFFS TO THE SEA

The resourceful inhabitants of Kent have always used the materials available to them, and many of these were to be found on the seashore. To get to and from the seashore around the Isle of Thanet, a series of gaps wide enough for a man, his mate and a waggon to pass along were excavated or widened. Sixteen in total were in use between Pegwell Bay and Westgate, to the west of Margate, called gates, gaps or stairs; the names Dumpton Gap, Broadstairs and Westgate are still in use today. The gap known as St Bartholemew's Gate was renamed King's Gate after it was used by King Charles II in 1683.

These were used to haul gravel and stones up to the higher ground, but more especially to harvest seaweed from the sea, for use as fertiliser on the land or to be burnt, powdered and exported to Holland for use in the ceramics industry.

These cuts through the chalk were eventually marked by stone gateways that could be closed off when invasion threatened.

GAVELKIND: THE ANCIENT LAW OF PARTIBLE INHERITANCE

The laws of Gavelkind were brought to Kent by the invading Jutes, who came from the continent with the Angles and Saxons, and were not rescinded until 1923.

One unusual law was the practice of partible inheritance, under which many people could inherit the wealth of someone who died without a will. This contrasted with the rule of primogeniture that covered the rest of Britain, where only the eldest inherited. The youngest person in the family benefitted most from this system, when a house was divided amongst a man's children; the youngest person was always allowed the part of the house with the hearth, as they were most in need of its warmth.

Partly due to this law, under which the land was divided into smaller and smaller units, Kent was never subject to the open field system of agriculture that predominated in other parts of the country, where common land is farmed in rotation by different villagers. In Kent, each man jealously guarded his own land, keeping it within the family.

The gavelkind laws also allowed a wife to inherit half her husband's estate on his death, whereas in other parts of the country it could be as low as one third. The innocent relatives of those accused of criminal activity also benefitted; in other parts of Britain a felon's lands were forfeit to the king, but in Kent it was passed to his (or her) descendants.

GIFTS FROM THE FRENCH: THE WINE OF ST THOMAS AND THE LOST RUBY OF FRANCE

The River Stour was once tidal as far as the village of Fordwich, which grew to become the main port for the city of Canterbury. The facilities of the small port were of such importance to the commerce of the city that when King Louis VII of France made a gift of 1,600 gallons of wine to Christ Church Priory, they paid some of this to the Mayor of Fordwich for the continued use of the crane that loaded and unloaded the ships.

King Louis had visited Canterbury and prayed at the shrine of St Thomas à Becket for his sick son, who had subsequently recovered, so the wine was known as 'The Wine of St Thomas'. Interestingly, an audit of the accounts of the priory, carried out in the mid-twentieth century, revealed that a sum of 40*s* was still being paid. I believe this has now been rectified.

A greater mystery associated with King Louis, however, is the fate of the Regale of France, a huge ruby that was considered at the time to be the greatest gem in Europe. The gift was included in his offerings at the shrine of St Thomas à Becket and when this was sacked by Henry VIII, the ruby made its way into Henry's private collection, becoming one of his favourites. On his death, the ruby mysteriously disappeared; it did not appear in the inventory of his belongings, nor subsequently in any royal inventory.

An entry in *Notes and Queries* of 1863 tells us that Henry's tomb was opened during the reign of George IV for the express reason of finding the stone. The search was not successful, and to this day the location of the Regale is still unknown.

GOAL RUNNING: SADLY NO LONGER PLAYED

The old Kentish sport of goal running has now died out, and is only remembered in the fond memories of its oldest residents. The earliest references to the game come from the beginning of the eighteenth century, and describe it as similar to an adult form of tag rugby.

The game was played on any open area or field and between sides of almost any size, although at a formal match, a number below thirty was usually agreed. The game was played barefoot, but club colours were usually adopted for match games. A goal line was set up with a flag at each end, one per team. The runner ran forwards towards a turning post located in the middle of the field (one per team) and had to return to base without being caught or 'tagged' by a member of the other team. The sport developed, and by the twentieth century, players were required to run around both turning posts (now flag posts) before returning to the goal line, and play was scored on points rather than touches.

Clubs were often sponsored by local landowners, who gave the use of their fields and provided money for refreshments afterwards, but this was gradually superseded by business sponsorship, such as the money put up by a local brewer for The Style & Winch Shield.

Teams disbanded in 1914 with the outbreak of the First World War and many re-formed again between the wars, but the time for such sport had passed and by the end of the Second World War it had all but disappeared.

GOODENING: A PRE-CHRISTMAS BONUS FOR WIDOWS

Writing in 1896, P.H. Ditchfield tells us that the ancient custom of 'going a-goodening' was still practiced in the little village of Newington-by-Sittingbourne, and probably in many more across the county.

On 21 December, St Thomas' Day, the widows of the parish visited the more well-to-do houses and repeated the phrase 'remember the goodening', upon which they were given small gifts of money. The women from Newington met at the White Hart Inn at the end of the day and divided the collection between them, a practice that would have been repeated in other villages across the county.

THE GREAT DOGG OF TROTTISCLIFFE: STILL OUT THERE

The Great Dogg of Trottiscliffe (pronounced Trosley) was first described in the nineteenth century by Charles Igglesden in his book *Saunters in Kent*, where he records several incidents of the dog attacking and sometimes killing travellers. This animal could have been an escaped big cat, or it could be the same ghostly grey dog described by other writers in the Maidstone area. Perhaps we'll never know.

THE GREEN MAN OF KENT: A PAGAN MYSTERY

Despite being a pagan symbol, the Green Man has been incorporated into the fabric of churches across the county; Canterbury and Rochester Cathedrals alone hold 120 Green Men symbols between them.

A Green Man.

The Green Man comes in several forms, including the unusual half-man half-cat seen at the church in Charing. Green Man symbols are also hidden in artistic greenery in various churches – in Whitstable they hide within the leafy carvings on the wooden pews, while in Patrixbourne they can be seen on the panels of the stained-glass windows.

There are also many examples of green animals. There are two lions in the Black Prince Chapel in Canterbury Cathedral, a green pig in Wye, a bull and a lion in Rochester Cathedral and a dragon in Stone, near Dartford.

Almost all the Green Men in Kent are sympathetic characters, but one is not so friendly. The Wild Man or woodwose depicted on a misericord in Faversham has a distinctly wild look about him.

THE GRETNA GREEN OF KENT: SO MANY MARRIAGES!

The tiny church of St Lawrence at Allington, which has now been replaced by a newer building, had seating for only twenty-nine parishioners and it became notorious in the seventeenth century for the practice of allowing marriages that may have been questioned in any other church.

Before the publishing of banns was made law, the incumbent of St Lawrence was known to be generous in his ratification of marriage applications, and couples came from far and wide to avail themselves of this generosity. The parish was as small as the church, with not many more than sixty people living there at any one time, but in 1651, for example, thirty-eight marriages were recorded.

The unusually high number of marriages ended when a law was passed that required banns to be posted in a public place, giving friends and families time to stop ill-considered unions.

GROTTOES AND GROTTERS: A KENTISH TRADITION

It was once commonplace for children around the Kent coast to create fantastic grottoes from a variety of shiny, unusual or otherwise interesting objects. Many of the grottoes featured shells or sea glass found on the nearby beaches, especially those constructed on or nearby the seafront, and children would show off their grottoes to passers-by and ask for small change with the cry 'Remember the grotter!', in the same way that children once asked for 'a penny for the guy'.

In London, and along the north Kent coast, children would take advantage of the beginning of the oyster season each August and build fanciful cairns or grottoes of discarded oyster shells, lighting each one with a candle. An empty shell might be used to collect the pennies that were donated.

The practice eventually fell from favour in the 1960s, but has been revived in Whitstable where children are shown how to make grottoes during the annual Oyster Festival. To add excitement to the event, it is the custom for each small cairn of oyster shells to be built around an electric tealight or small torch, and the beach takes on a magical appearance when they are all lit at the end of the day.

A GUN-TOTING LANDLADY: RINGLESTONE'S OWN ANNIE OAKLEY

The Ringlestone Inn at Harrietsham was taken over in the mid-1950s by Mrs Gasking and her daughter Dora. Everything went well until it became the popular haunt of gangs of youths on motorbikes, although most of them treated the place with respect, and affectionately called Mrs Gasking 'Ma'. However, one evening in 1963, after a busy Bank Holiday, things got out of hand and when a window was broken, Ma had had enough. She fetched a shotgun filled with blanks and fired over the heads of the revellers, an event that made the national news.

Bikers still turned up at the pub, despite Ma's temper and rules for the bar becoming more and more stringent, and in 1966 she sold up and retired.

GURU NANAK DARBAR GURDWARA: A LITTLE BIT OF INDIA IN NORTH-WEST KENT

The first Sikhs arrived in Kent in the 1950s and the number grew quickly over the next decade or so. Settling in the Gravesend area, they were welcomed by the local community, as Canterbury had welcomed the Huguenots, Sandwich the Walloons, and Folkestone the Belgians. The Sikh community now accounts for about 15 per cent of the population in the Gravesham area.

The Gravesend gurdwara, or temple, is named after Guru Nanak Sahib Ji, the founder of Sikhism, and was opened in 2010. The design was inspired by Indian architecture, but also reflects the lifestyles of those it serves in modern-day Kent. The building includes prayer halls and dining rooms, and has its own lecture hall, library, kitchen, nursery and a day centre for the elderly.

The regular open days held at the gurdwara give the people of Kent a chance to experience the culture and generosity of the Sikh community.

GYPSY TART: KENTISH KITCHEN ALCHEMY

Kent is famous for many of its foods, and is almost synonymous with hops, oysters and Dover sole. However, it is perhaps the gypsy tart that most people will remember from any visit to the county.

Rich, delicious, and brimming with calories, the gypsy tart is a favourite with children and adults alike. This simple recipe contains just three ingredients: pastry, sugar and evaporated milk, which are magically transformed during the cooking process into a tart with a soft yet firm consistency that is hard to resist.

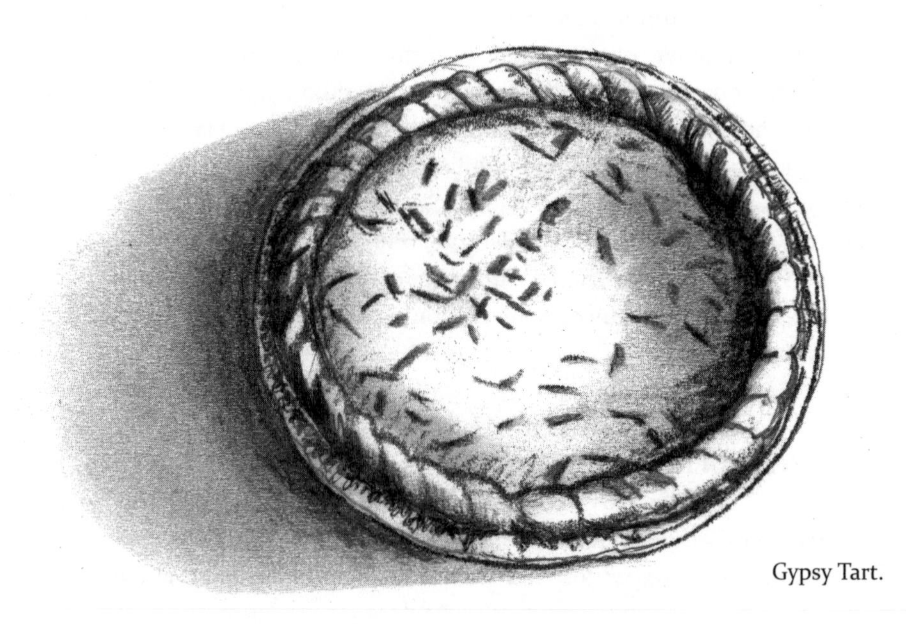

Gypsy Tart.

H

HADLOW TOWER:
THE TALLEST VICTORIAN FOLLY IN ENGLAND

Hadlow Tower, located near Tonbridge, is also known as May's Folly, as it was built by Walter Barton May as part of a much larger estate. The house and gardens have long since gone but the tower remains, standing lonely on its own, and is now famous as the tallest folly in the country, higher even than Nelson's Column.

It is said that May built the tower so that he could spy on his wife if and when she met their neighbour for a 'dalliance'. This may have been a rumour spread by gossips, but it seems May was intent on getting the building completed, even though he was nearly made bankrupt in the process. After his death, his son was forced to sell the property to pay his father's debts and the building is now a private residence.

What a sad end to what could have so easily been one of the greatest romantic gestures of all time.

HARMSWORTH'S ALLIGATOR:
KEEPING WARM IN THE CONSERVATORY

Alfred Harmsworth, Viscount Northcliffe, was the founder of the *Daily Mail* who, after acquiring *The Observer*, *The Times* and *The Sunday Times*, eventually controlled over 40 per cent of the British press. He kept horses, but was also fascinated by motor vehicles and was one of the first motorists to take part in the London to Brighton Run.

Harmsworth's house at Broadstairs was called Elmwood, and it sat on a large estate, which he extended to cover 250 acres. The house was modernised and updated, taking account of all the modern trends, and became a magnet for the rich and famous; Mary Pickford and Douglas Fairbanks honeymooned at the house. Out of all the destinations in the world, Hollywood royalty chose Kent!

Also living on the estate were Harmsworth's beloved animals, among which were several prize pigs and a pet alligator. There is very little information about the alligator to be found, but it reportedly spent its winters in the Clock House Conservatory in Broadstairs, trying to keep warm.

HEART SHRINES: A REMINDER OF THE CRUSADES

When a person died away from home in the twelfth century, it was often impractical to transport the body back for burial, so a sample was taken home to the relatives for interment, which was often the heart. This could be encased in silver, ivory or lead for transport, and buried with full honours once home.

There are about thirty such burials across the UK, and Kent has two documented examples, the best of which is at Leysbourne, which is an unusual double shrine, believed to be that of Sir Roger of Leybourne and his wife.

Another shrine, at Brabourne, made of Bethersden marble, contains the heart of John Balliol, founder of Balliol College, Oxford, placed there after the death of his wife, who had previously had the heart embalmed and kept it with her.

The existence of other shrines, such as that at Fordwich, is apocryphal, although more may have been hidden during subsequent church restoration work and may lie waiting to be discovered.

THE HERONS OF CHILHAM CASTLE: HARBINGERS OF DISASTER

The Norman castle at Chilham was built soon after the invasion of William I, and inhabited by a succession of owners. By the time Sir Dudley Digges bought it in the early seventeenth century, it was sadly in need of updating and in 1616 he built a modern manor house on the site (*see* Dudley Digges and the Running Field). He incorporated the Norman tower into his design and it is now one of the oldest continually inhabited buildings in the country.

The large house and grounds have changed hands many times and are currently flourishing, but legend has it that if the herons fail to roost by St Valentine's Day, 14 February, disaster will strike the family. Herons were, in fact, once kept in a heronry at the castle during the thirteenth century, in much the same as a modern farmer might keep a flock of turkeys for the table. Although this no longer exists, the birds still visit the ornamental lake, ensuring the continuation of the estate.

The village sign of Chilham still shows a heron.

Another possible derivation of the legend is revealed when we understand that a family by the name of Heron owned Chilham Castle in the seventeenth century. The legend could have been created in reference to the ruling family, and not the bird. Nonetheless, the herons are staying in the gardens. Just in case.

HEVER'S TUDOR COTTAGES: REAL OR REPLICA?

Although Hever Castle was home to two Tudor queens, the Tudor-style guest cottages were constructed in the twentieth century. The buildings were the brainchild of William Waldorf Astor, and he even changed the course of the River Eden during the work, to accommodate them.

Beautifully designed to look like a series of homes from throughout the Tudor period, the cottages have been built in traditional fashion from timber, lathe and plaster, and workers even used authentic Tudor tools in their construction. The 100 rooms are linked by a series of passages to make the space more flexible, and are known as the Astor Wing rather than as individual premises.

THE HOLY MAID OF KENT: HER VISIONS WERE HER UNDOING

Elizabeth Barton was born in a village near Aldington and worked as a servant girl at Court Lodge Farm, a manor house that had been bought by Henry VII and much extended. About 1525 she became ill and as a result of this had times when she fell into trances that reportedly contained religious visions. Three years later, she entered a nunnery in Canterbury, but the visions did not stop and she became known as the Holy Maid of Kent.

Unfortunately for Elizabeth, the visions told her that she should warn Henry VIII that if he divorced Katherine of Aragon and married Anne Boleyn the vengeance of God would fall upon him and he would die within months. She did manage to gain an audience with Henry and warned him of her prophecies, which failed to come true when he married Anne. Elizabeth quickly changed her prophecy from death for Henry to removal from the throne.

Not surprisingly, she was tried for treason, found guilty, and hanged at Tyburn in April 1534. She is remembered as being the only woman whose head was displayed on a spike on London Bridge.

THE HOODENERS OF EAST KENT: UNLIKE ANY OTHER CHRISTMAS TRADITION IN ENGLAND

The representation of a horse in ancient ritualistic plays is not unique to Kent, but the character made by men across east Kent varies from those in other parts of the UK, and indeed from the west of Kent, where players performed Miracle or Mystery Plays as part of their Christmas celebrations. The Kentish Hooden Horse does not have the skull of a horse mounted on a pole, but is a less macabre, more fun-filled incarnation, with the longest traditions coming from the Isle of Thanet.

It is said that the Hooden Horse was brought to Kent by the Jutes, those lesser-known invaders who came to our shores at the same time as the Saxons and the Angles, and the man depicting the horse itself was the Hoodener.

The Hooden Hose comes with his own retinue of supporting characters, but the story is without words. The Rider attempts to mount the Horse, the Waggoner leads the parade and cracks his whip at the Horse, the Molly (a character like a pantomime dame) bustles along, sweeping as she goes, no doubt 'accidentally' sweeping the nearest members of the audience. In the nineteenth century, the Molly often had a blackened face, possibly to disguise the identity of the man playing her.

As far as we know, the Horse and his entourage were once used by field hands much as the figure of Guy Fawkes was used in the old Penny-for-the-Guy scenario. Men, often those who worked with horses in the fields, would create a rudimentary horse from a piece of sacking, a pole and a head with a snapping wooden jaw. More sophisticated versions had manes, leather ears and painted features. The hinged wooden jaw, however crude, could be clacked together, startling passers-by and onlookers into astonishment that would segue into laughter.

Taken round the neighbourhood in the evenings, it is easy to see how the spectacle could be unsettling, to say the least, especially if, as sometimes happened, nails had been inserted into the jaw to represent teeth. Each Christmas, the group, along with as many musicians as could be mustered, travelled through the village from house to house, demanding cakes and ale where they could be obtained, entertaining as they went.

The practice was banned in the nineteenth century as it developed into something unpleasantly bawdy, but has now resurfaced, often as part of the traditional Morris troupe repertoire.

HUFFLERS AND HOVELLERS: SEEN ON THE EAST KENT COAST

These are both names that are applied to either the man employed in the work or his vessel. Both work on the north and east coasts of Kent.

A hoveller is the name for a sturdy open clinker-built boat that can be rowed through the stormiest of seas to help vessels in distress and also for the man who does this work. It is interesting to find accounts of hovellers both as rescuers and as scavengers. There is little or no evidence to suggest they actually caused wrecks, but they certainly availed themselves of the opportunity to scavenge from a wreck once the crew had been saved. The men undertaking this work were unlicensed.

The work of a huffler was more regulated, as they were working much nearer to London, on the Thames Estuary rather than in the rough North Sea. The work of the huffler was to ferry goods from the chandler to waiting ships and barges, so they didn't need to wait for the tide to come in. The name is immortalised in the pub The Hufflers Arms in Dartford. The name was also applied to a boat working as a dredger at Sandwich, which would have been crewed by five or six men at a time.

I

IGUANODON: THE SYMBOL OF MAIDSTONE

The Iguanodon seems an unlikely choice of mascot for a thriving county town, and yet the worthy burghers of Maidstone have chosen one to represent their town, and 'Iggy' appears proudly on the town's coat of arms.

The reason lies in the fact that an Iguanodon was one of the first residents of Maidstone. His fossilised remains were dug up in 1834 in Queen's Road and were quickly taken into the hearts of the Maidstone locals.

Iggy, as he became known, had lain beneath the town for over 120 million years, and had weighed up to 5 tons before his death, surprising scientists who had expected him to be much smaller. Due to his importance as a national treasure, Iggy now lives in the Natural History Museum, but casts of his bones are on display at the Maidstone Museum.

Iggy was not added to the Maidstone Borough Council coat of arms until 1946, but is now recognised as an integral part of the history of the area and deserving of such an honour. He is the only dinosaur to have his image included in a coat of arms.

THE INFERNAL DIVER: INVENTOR OF THE FIREMAN'S HELMET AND THE DIVING SUIT

Visitors to Whitstable might be surprised to see a Banksy-style work by local artist Catman as they turn into Oxford Street, which depicts a man in an old-fashioned diving suit carrying bags of shopping.

As it happens, Whitstable is forever linked with the diving fraternity due to the Deane brothers, who invented the first diving helmet.

John Deane was the first to develop the idea, when he witnessed a stable fire during the 1820s. Grabbing the helmet from a suit of armour, he asked the attendant firemen to pump air into the helmet instead of pumping water at the fire. Using this system, he was able to rescue the horses and patented his invention as an 'Apparatus or Machine to be worn by Persons entering Rooms or other places filled with Smoke or other Vapour, for the purpose of extinguishing Fire, or extricating Persons or Property therein'.

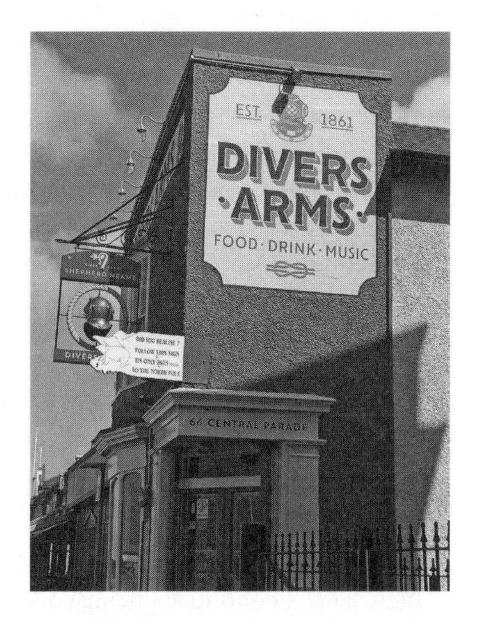

The Diver's Arms in Herne Bay, showing an original helmet on the pub sign.

Further work on the design saw the birth of the first diving helmet and later the diving suit called Deane's Patent Diving Dress, which were both tested off the coast of Whitstable. The brothers worked all around the coast, including in the English Channel, where, in 1836, they discovered the location of the *Mary Rose*, Henry VIII's ill-fated gunship.

After his brother's death, John continued to work as a diver, including work in the Black Sea during the Crimean War. It was during this conflict that he earned the nickname 'The Infernal Diver', from a correspondent of *The Times* newspaper, who used the expression following an explosion caused by Deane.

John married into a local Whitstable family and continued to live in the area until his death, aged 84.

THE INGOLDSBY LEGENDS: TALES FROM THE FIFTH CONTINENT

The Ingoldsby Legends were a series of short stories written by Richard Barham under the pen name Thomas Ingoldsby.

Barham was a vicar living on the Romney Marsh at the beginning of the nineteenth century, and drew heavily on his Canterbury childhood and the lives of the people around him to give credence to his stories. It was his ability to include real people and places in the tales that gave them their charm, and led many people to believe they were true events from the history of Kent. The stories are packed with details of smuggling exploits, murders and ghosts that have a real ring of truth about them, although they are, of course, purely fictional.

The Ingoldsby Legends were terrifically popular in their day, and are still read, although not so widely. It was Richard Barham who introduced the concept of the Romney Marsh area as somewhere quite separate from the rest of the world, dubbing it 'the fifth continent'.

INLAND PORTS: UNLIKELY, BUT TRUE

Bounded on three sides by water, the coast of Kent is constantly changing with erosion and floods, storms and man-made diversions altering the outline of the county and the course of rivers through the mainland.

New land is continually being added, by longshore drift at Dungeness, by land reclamation of marshes in both the north and south of the county and, most amazingly, by the addition of a whole nature reserve at Samphire Hoe, built with the spoil from the Channel Tunnel excavations. The town of New Romney was so named because Old Romney was silted up and it was no longer possible to use it as a port.

These changes to the landscape have led to the formation of new industries, but also to the loss of others.

Fordwich

The tiny village of Fordwich was once of such importance to the neighbouring city of Canterbury that it was granted status as a port and a town. Fordwich was the highest navigable point up the River Stour where ships could bring goods and passengers from the continent in to Canterbury, and the old Court Hall built in the Middle Ages is still used by the Town Council, making it one of the oldest and smallest Town Halls in the country. The lower rooms were once used as a prison and storehouse, while the upper room constituted a jury room and a courtroom.

Crane House, a later addition, was the site of the crane used to load and unload the sailing ships that waited for the tides, but was also used to punish women who overstepped the mark. This was not a test for witchcraft, as some have suggested, but a quick dip in the river while strapped to a chair was merely a warning to those troublesome women who ignored verbal warnings from the worthies of the town. The wooden chair can still be seen in the Court Hall Museum.

Fordwich lost its status as a town in 1883, but still has a Town Council and still draws tourists who visit the Court Hall and wonder that a village so far inland was once so important to the economic growth of the area.

Smallhythe

Another of Kent's inland ports is the village of Smallhythe, which was once a notable shipyard and the port that served the town of Tenderden. Smallhythe stood on the River Rother until the storm of 1636, which changed the course of the river and altered the fortunes of many who lived in the south of Kent. Those who made their livings in the marine industry found themselves suddenly living far away from the sea, as the mouth of the Rother now lay at Rye instead of New Romney.

The decline of shipbuilding in the area was slow, however, and ships were built at Smallhythe until the reign of Henry VIII, and smaller cargoes were still carried up the much-reduced river channel. This is borne out by the fact that the Harbourmasters House was built in about 1515, showing that the post was still extant at this time.

IVOREX: THE CRAZE THAT SWEPT THE WORLD

Arthur Osborne was born in Ospringe, near Faversham, in 1855, and showed a talent for arts and crafts early in his life. After attending South Kensington School of Art, he emigrated to Canada and, later, to America, but returned in 1898 to live and work in Faversham.

Osborne opened a factory producing fancy goods and he soon perfected the art of creating a product he called Ivorex, which became famous worldwide as well as a major employer in the area.

Each Ivorex plaque was essentially a relief plaster cast of a famous landmark or historical event, which was sealed with paraffin wax after it had been painted. The soft creamy sheen of the material gave the product its name. Osborne himself created the clay master moulds for the plaques, working from photographs and postcards of popular destinations and monuments, including scenes from new novels such as those of Charles Dickens.

The Ivorex factory created up to 1,000 different subjects, although many were designed for private buyers and never entered into the catalogue. The plaques were sold in great numbers, and at the height of their popularity 45,000 pieces were made each year to be sold in the UK and around the world. The quality of Ivorex plaques was so high that they were exhibited at the Royal Academy and in the Empire Exhibition of 1924.

As with all crazes, the market eventually dwindled, and with the advent of the Second World War, sales dropped dramatically. Arthur Osborne died in 1943, and although the company continued until 1965, the pre-war sales figures were never regained. The moulds were purchased by Bossons, who used them to produce plaques, but genuine Osborne Ivorex items, made in Kent, are stamped AO.

This is one more example of a genuinely Kentish invention that became a global phenomenon (*see* OXO, Sharp's Toffee and Subbuteo). This tiny corner of the country has added more than its fair share of iconic items to the British household.

An Ivorex plaque.

JACK-IN-THE-GREEN: REVIVED IN ROCHESTER

The character of Jack-in-the-Green has only been around for just over 150 years, but the tradition upon which he is built goes back into the mists of time. Jack is associated with the trade of sweeping chimneys, and was created to celebrate their trade. Jack consists of a peculiar wicker frame covered with greenery, with a man on the inside to guide it; he wears a crown of leaves and flowers on his head.

Both Whitstable and Rochester have a history of Jack-in-the-Green celebrations, which are now generally seen on the late May bank holiday instead of being part of the May Day celebrations, which was a holiday for sweeps, giving them the opportunity for revelry, and Hever Castle has also started a Jack-in-the-Green festival.

The celebration in Rochester is linked to Morris dancers, and to the Sweeps Festival, so many people dress as sweeps with brooms and blackened faces for the day. The character of Jack is taken from *Sketches by Boz*, written by Kent author Charles Dickens; he is surrounded by twelve bonfires and woken by Morris dancers.

JAMES BOND: INTERNATIONAL MAN OF MYSTERY

James Bond's creator, Ian Fleming, had a holiday home at St Margaret's Bay, at the foot of the white cliffs and with a toe in the English Channel. The first book to feature the Kent coast and its inhabitants was *Moonraker*, with a large part of the action taking place from Thanet all the way down to Dover, where the beams of the South Goodwin Lighthouse are thrown across the cliffs.

The action in *Goldfinger* was set slightly further north, including Reculver and Ramsgate – Goldfinger's company is even called Thanet Alloy Research. Ian Fleming was not born in Kent, nor did he spend much time here, but he did love golf and created St Mark's Golf Course for his books, based almost entirely on the Royal St George's Golf Course at Sandwich, where Bond famously played a round with his nemesis Auric Goldfinger.

Fleming also spent time at The Duck Inn, in Pett Bottom, where he wrote a large proportion of *You Only Live Twice*. The action of the novel is not set in Kent, but Bond does talk about his childhood home near The Duck. It is a popular local fact that the No. 7 bus travelled past the pub on its way to London, and it is said that this inspired James Bond's iconic number, 007.

JAMES II: CATCH OF THE DAY

William of Orange came to England in 1688 to take the throne from James II, with huge support from the people of England who preferred the Anglican William and his wife Mary to the Roman Catholic James. James tried to flee, but was captured by a group of Faversham fishermen before he could leave the country.

The king had disguised himself as a servant and travelled along the north Kent coast to board a fishing boat at Elmley Island. Their departure was delayed by bad weather, and as midnight approached, they were set upon by the Faversham fishermen. The rumour mill, well-oiled by the smuggling trade, had passed on information about a party of rich merchants gathered at Elmley, and the fishermen had come to find out what was going on, hoping they could relieve them of some of their wealth. They robbed the men, decided that there might possibly be a reward for their capture, and took them back to Faversham. There the unfortunate monarch and his men were taken to the Queen's Head pub, where they were recognised and, in a quick volte-face, treated to dinner at the house of the Mayor.

Far from leaving the country quietly, James was picked up by a contingent of lifeguards and taken to Rochester, and thence to London. After a magnificent feast, and much hand-shaking, the king was again taken to Rochester, just a week after his arrest at Elmley, this time accompanied by the Dutch Guards of William and Mary. The gaolers looked the other way, and James made his escape, once again travelling along the north Kent coast. James boarded a ship at Shellness on the Isle of Sheppey and escaped quietly to France to join his family, avoiding further battles.

The last bizarre fact in this farcical tale is the fact that James never forgot the role of the fishermen from Faversham who treated him so roughly. When he issued a royal pardon, he specifically excluded the fishermen of Faversham, meaning that they have never been forgiven for their treatment of the royal personage.

JARS IN THE WALLS: MYSTERIOUS VESSELS IN THE WALLS OF CHURCHES

The church of St Clements in Sandwich has vessels built into the walls in the chancel, near the altar, and three jars were found in the gables of the church of St Nicholas in Newington.

It has been found that many churches have jars that remain hidden, or have been removed; the church at Leeds was home to approximately fifty jars, running the whole length of the nave, which have been removed and can now be seen in Maidstone Museum.

Scholars and academics are still unsure why they were included in the fabrication of the buildings, although it is possible that they were laid with their necks visible to improve the acoustics of the building.

JESSE SPICER: KILLED BY A NINE-PIN BOWL

The village of Pluckley is known as the most haunted village in the country, and yet amongst all the hype and hyperbole lies a real human tragedy.

Poor Jesse Spicer was having a great evening at his local pub, the Black Horse Inn, when he suffered a freak accident – he was struck with a ball from the game of nine-pin bowls that was being played. At just 27 years of age and with a wife and three children at home, Jesse died and was buried in the Pluckley cemetery in 1772.

JOE SPECKS: STRANGER THAN FICTION

An impressive carved stone inscription above the Oxfam bookshop in Rochester High Street informs us that the building was the home of Joe Specks. Visitors might wonder about Joe and the wonderful contributions to humanity that had warranted such a memorial.

In fact, such a traveller would do well to remember the high esteem in which the city of Rochester holds Mr Charles Dickens, for Joe Specks was not a living being, but a character in the book *The Uncommercial Traveller*. The memorial was erected in 1928, and stands today as a mark of the regard the city holds, not for Joe Specks, but for his creator, Charles Dickens.

JOSEPH CROOMBE PETIT: THE HERMIT OF DUMPTON CAVE

The little village of Dumpton, now subsumed into the town of Ramsgate, was once a quiet and leafy backwater. Behind a dilapidated old manor house, was a cave hollowed out of the escarpment, in which Joseph Croombe Petit made his home.

Elizabeth Strutt, writing in 1823, describes for us the beauty of the spot, and tells us that Joseph had of his own free will gone to live in the cave in order to prepare himself for death by simple living and religious contemplation.

Joseph had been born at Wingham in 1742. He had been a plasterer by trade, specialising in ornamental plasterwork, but after working in many counties across the south of England he had sustained a head injury that had forced him to retire. The severity of the injury had led doctors to subject him to trepanning, a procedure whereby a hole was drilled into the skull in the hope of relieving any build-up of pressure. As a result, he always wore a blue headscarf around his head.

The small cave was filled with everything one might expect in a cottage, and even had paper on the walls. Strutt explains that living in such a way was not uncommon among the inhabitants of Thanet. Joseph had a small income from the laces and garters that he made and sold locally, and he lived a frugal, vegetarian life.

Joseph was well known for his good works in the local area, and became something of a St Francis character, communing with birds, bringing comfort to the afflicted and ministering to the sick. He also took practical steps to help people, and frequently took a collection for those in most dire need.

I have been unable to find out the fate of 'The Hermit of Dumpton', but knowing how he was well-loved by the people he visited, I can only hope he was well looked after when he was unable to do so for himself.

A JOURNEY TO JAPAN: THE LEGEND OF THE SHOGUN

At the beginning of the seventeenth century, Portugal had sole trading rights with Japan, and other countries coveted these privileges. In 1598, 34-year-old William

Adams, having retired from the Royal Navy, joined a Dutch trading expedition and arrived two years later on the shores of Japan. He was immediately imprisoned at the behest of the Portuguese, who were reluctant to allow a Protestant into the country, but he was quickly released when the Japanese realised that his navigation and shipbuilding skills could be of use to them.

Adams lived in Japan for the next twenty years, changing his name to Miura Angin and even taking a Japanese wife by whom he had two children, but his death in 1620 signalled the end of trade with the country, which closed itself off from the West completely. He was the last Englishman to enter Japan for 250 years, and many readers may be familiar with his story as it was fictionalised into the popular television series *Shogun* in the 1980s.

A superb clock tower was erected in Gillingham in 1934 in his honour, which can be seen on the north side of the A2. The town of Ido in Japan also honours Adams with a festival called Anginsai, which was started in 1947 and continues to this day.

JUTES: OUR FOREBEARS AND ANCESTORS

After the Romans left Kent in AD 400, the whole infrastructure of day-to-day life in England gradually unravelled. The town of Canterbury seems to have been almost completely abandoned during this period, with the inhabitants maybe moving to London to cling to the lifestyle they had come to enjoy.

Without the Romans to lead them, political rumblings started throughout Britain as tribal chiefs started to gather armies and fight against each other, although they did eventually come together under Vortigern, the High King. To counter the threat of invasion from the Picts and the Scots, Bede tells us that Vortigern asked the Angles, Saxons and Jutes from Northern Germany and Denmark, to help. They came in AD 446, led by Hengist and Horsa, and landed near Richborough at Pegwell Bay, travelling across the sea in three longships; the broad bay offered an easy landing spot with its shallow, sheltered waters.

The mercenaries, seeing the disarray within Britain, fought their way across Kent and southern England, battling at Aylesford, Crayford and Ebbsfleet, taking control as they went. Eventually, they divided Britain between them. The Saxons took over Sussex, Wessex and Essex, the Angles took East Anglia, Mercia and Northumbria, and the Jutes (led by the Angles Hengist and Horsa) stayed in Kent, adopting the white horse as their symbol. (*See* Gavelkind.)

THE KENT DITCH: DIVIDING KENT FROM SUSSEX

It was the Romans who first started to reclaim land at Romney Marsh, adding sea defences and creating drainage systems. The marshes in the south of Kent have been repeatedly reclaimed and left to be covered by water, but have recently remained relatively stable, and are managed as natural resources and wildlife areas.

The Kent Ditch, although it has such an unprepossessing name, is an important drainage channel that runs along the border between the counties of Kent and Sussex. It was created in the fourteenth and fifteenth centuries as a method of controlling the water coming off the land and running into the River Rother. It is now part of a recognised wildlife corridor.

KENTISH CHERRY BRANDY: THE SECRET RECIPE STILL IN USE TODAY

In the middle of the nineteenth century, Thomas Grant took over his family's business and introduced cherry brandy into their range of products, blending local Morello cherries with brandy at the works in Limekiln Street, Dover. He eventually expanded into factories at Lenham and Maidstone. The cherries were grown for the company in the fields around Lenham and the Charing Heath area.

Another strong link with cherries is seen at The Crown Inn in Sarre, which is known as Cherry Brandy House, and is famous for its brandy made to a secret recipe brought to Kent by the Huguenot refugees fleeing persecution in France. Over 200 years later, survivors of the Charge of the Light Brigade held their reunion dinners at the inn. The brandy is said to be the most exclusive cherry brandy in the world, and is available only from The Crown Inn.

Cherry Brandy House, Sarre.

KENTISH FIRE: FROM HEATH TO TERRACES

Kentish Fire is not a type of combustion, nor a will-o'-the-wisp, but a kind of clapping!

Penenden Heath has long been associated with political uprisings, from the first recorded lawsuit between Odo, King of Kent, and Lanfranc, Bishop of Canterbury, through the gathering of men under Watt Tyler for the Peasants' Revolt, to the rebellion in 1554 against Queen Mary and on to the Battle of Maidstone, part of the English Civil War.

The day of the Shire Court in 1829 at which a petition was brought against the Catholic Relief Act must have been deafening to those around. The Act allowed members of the Roman Catholic Church to become members of Parliament, and 50,000 men gathered on the heath to debate the matter. The debate was heated, and it is said that the sound of Kentish Fire was heard for miles.

Kentish Fire has been described as a rhythmic clapping, consisting of two long claps followed by three shorter ones, similar to the refrain heard at football matches today, and was used to signal dissent. One can imagine that a few men might start to clap, showing their disagreement, and that the noise gradually rose to a crescendo as more and more people joined in, drowning out the speaker.

The rhythm may have been taken up by those drinking a toast, as the sound of the shot glass being banged upside down on the table is also known as 'fire'.

This practice was recorded in 1851 in the minutes of a Masons meeting as Kentish Fire, and this is possibly because it was done in the Kentish rhythm.

KENTISH MAN OR MAN OF KENT: A COUNTY DIVIDED

To an outsider, the phrases 'Man of Kent' or 'Kentish Man' may seem interchangeable, but to a man or woman born in the county, they are certainly not. The division between the two terms falls along the course of the River Medway, and although it is now a matter of friendly rivalry, it was once hotly contested.

When the Angles, Saxons and Jutes took over in AD 410, the Angles moved north, some of the Saxon mercenaries stayed in Kent, settling in the western villages, while the Jutes remained in the east of the county. It might be this Jute/Saxon split that gave rise to the differentiation between Men of Kent in the east and Kentish Men in the west. Differences in burial customs vary between east and west Kent, which also suggests to this division. Furthermore, there is evidence from documents of the time that there were in fact two Kings of Kent, as well as the fact that there are two cathedral cities.

So when you meet a person from the county of Kent, remember that if you call them a Man or Maid of Kent when they are actually a Kentish Man or a Kentish Maid, you could be causing offence. Tread carefully!

KING LOUIS OF ENGLAND: WHAT THE HISTORY BOOKS WILL NEVER TELL YOU

When King John, known as John Lackland, came to the throne in 1199, a band of rebel barons tried to take the throne as they did not trust him to keep to the spirit of the Magna Carta. The first uprising in 1215 ended in the siege of Rochester Castle where the barons were held for over six weeks. Eventually the soldiers of the Crown dug tunnels underneath the south-eastern tower, which collapsed when the wooden props were deliberately burnt down, allegedly with the fat of forty pigs.

The barons then invited Louis VIII of France to take the throne. He landed at Thanet, and arrived in London in June, where he announced that he was King of England. Although never officially crowned, he effectively ruled England for eighteen months, until his battle fleet was defeated at Sandwich in 1217 (*see* The Battle of Sandwich). Louis departed and Henry III took the throne.

KIT MARLOWE: KNIFE CRIME IN DEPTFORD

Christopher Marlowe was born in Kent, educated in Canterbury and Cambridge, and died in Deptford. Between these bare facts, however, lies a web of unknown facts and mysteries.

Kit, as he was known, was the son of a shoemaker, who was rich enough to send his son to the Kings School in Canterbury, and then to Cambridge. By the age of 22, Kit had written and found a publisher for his first play, and over the next seven years he wrote six more major works of literature.

It is widely believed that he led a double life, working as a spy for Elizabeth I in between writing his plays, although there is tantalizingly little evidence for this. His religious views would undoubtedly have been cause for concern, as he read widely and baited friends with outspoken opinions on both Roman Catholicism and atheism, a stance that was considered to be as serious as treason at that time.

Marlowe was arrested for blasphemy in 1593, but was allowed to leave court on payment of bail, and a few days later, at the age of just 29, he was stabbed to death in Deptford, leaving a bewildered public to guess at the motive of the attack and to decide whether it was an assassination or aggravated manslaughter.

The court rolls show the skill of the lawyers, and Ingram Frizer who stabbed Marlowe, pleaded self-defence and was pardoned by the Queen just two weeks later. It has been suggested that Frizer was also a spy and had either been engaged to kill Marlowe or to gather information from him.

Scholars and criminologists alike have tried to fathom the reason for Marlowe's early death, and failed to solve the riddle. It seems likely that we will never know what happened that night, in a passage behind Mrs Bull's alehouse in the heart of Deptford.

THE KITCHENER CAMP FOR REFUGEES: A LIFESAVER FOR GERMAN JEWS

Passing along the quiet back roads from Sandwich to the Discovery Park Business Centre, it is hard to imagine that eighty years ago the village of Stonar would have been a hive of activity, with pedestrians and motor vehicles coming and going between the village and the town of Sandwich.

During the first years of Hitler's persecution of the German Jews, many fled to England, seeking asylum. The site at Stonar, a former army camp, was adapted by the Council of German Jewry to house Jewish men from Germany,

Czechoslovakia and Austria who had been released from concentration camps on the proviso that they would leave Germany immediately. Almost 5,000 men arrived and were housed in barrack-like huts.

Later, many arranged for their wives and children to join them and the camp developed into a self-contained village, where people traded with each other and with the residents of Sandwich. One by one, family by family, the refugees found work either in the UK or in another country, and moved away. By the end of the war, fewer than 1,000 remained and these were relocated further from the coast.

KIT'S COTY HOUSE: A NAME LOST IN TIME

Even the brightest academics have no idea who Kit was or what a Coty House is. The name refers to a dolmen burial site near the River Medway, and the stones, which resemble a small house, are at the entrance to a large underground tomb.

The burial site was constructed during the New Stone Age, and is the sister site to Little Kit's Coty House, which has been dismantled. (*See* The Countless Stones.)

The monument is made of sarsen stone, as are parts of Stonehenge, and most of it has been eroded away over time. The three upright stones, capped by a large flat stone, formed the entrance to the earthwork which stretched backwards from it like a huge Neolithic Anderson shelter.

The site is evocative, and as the land around it is largely undeveloped, it is possible to stand quietly and feel the lives of those who went before whisper in your ear.

Kit's Coty House.

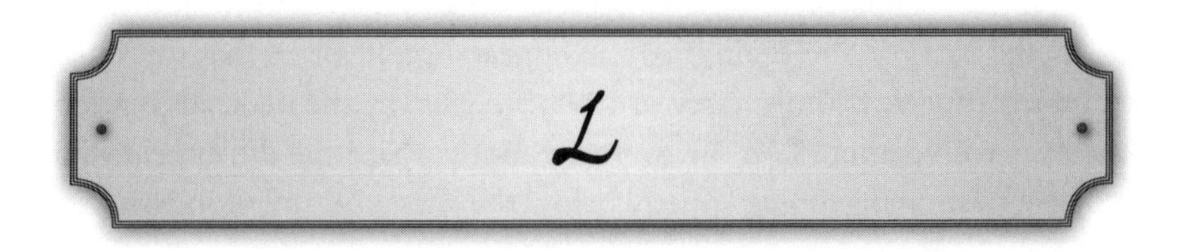

THE LADY IN THE WOODS: A FORGOTTEN SCULPTURE

Like the Mona Lisa, the Lady in the Woods seems to harbour a secret. The sculpture is almost hidden in Kite Hill Wood near Stalisfield Green, and stands waiting for the birth of her child, locked in contemplation beneath the trees.

Made of oak, and nearly 9ft tall, it seems unbelievable that the origin of the statue remains unknown. Nobody knows who carved her, nor even how long she has been waiting in the woods.

Despite regular reports in the local press, nobody has ever come forward to be acknowledged as her creator, nor been able to shed any light on the woman who was the inspiration for the piece. As time goes by, it is more and more unlikely that an answer will ever be found.

LADY LOVIBOND: A BEAUTY IN THE WATER

Lady Lovibond moves slowly and gracefully through the water, drawing the eyes of all who see her, however, *Lady Lovibond* is not a woman, but a ship.

Every eighteenth-century sailor knew that it was bad luck to have a woman on board, and when Captain Andrew Whalley declared himself unable to leave his new wife, Annetta, at home and that she would travel to Portugal aboard the *Lady Lovibond*, they knew their fate was sealed. As the ship left the Thames Estuary and moved southwards, Captain Whalley was attacked by his first mate in a jealous rage, and with no captain at the helm, the ship foundered and the treacherous Goodwin Sands claimed her. There are now more than 2,000 confirmed wrecks on the Goodwin Sands, but the *Lady Lovibond* is one of the best-remembered, not for the circumstances of her demise, but for what happened next.

The next part of the story begins fifty years later, when the ship was sighted by the captain of the *Edenbridge*, who recorded a near miss in his journal, and in 1898 and in 1948 she again made an appearance. It seems that she was not seen on her fifty-year anniversary in 1998, not even by the dedicated group of enthusiasts who gathered on the shoreline. But perhaps she did appear, sailing out of the mists and slipping quietly below the waves on the Goodwin Sands out of sight of those who waited.

The next sighting is due to take place on 13 February 2048, for those brave enough to look for the ghost ship that foundered for love.

LATHES AND SULUNGS: ANCIENT DIVISIONS OF LAND

Historically, Kent has always been divided into Lathes, from the Saxon word 'laethe' meaning 'land'. The seven lathes were Borowart and Estrel (jointly St Augustines), Middletune and Wiwarlet (jointly the Lathe of Scray), Limowart (Lymne, which became Shepway), Sudtone (Sutton-at-Hone), and Elesford (Aylesford).

Another uniquely Kentish term that appears in Domesday Book in connection with Kent is the sulung, which is a measure of land, and was larger than the usual measure, which was the curacate. A sulung was between 200 and 250 acres in size, but it is interesting to note that the enumerators of the Domesday Book used their knowledge of the land to denote 'size' dependent upon the quality of the soil or even the shape of the land under assessment.

Areas were further divided into Hundreds. A small village or group of ten households constituted a 'tithing' and ten of these (100 homes) made up a Hundred. Each Hundred had its own court and a constable to keep the peace. Households were required to pay one penny a year, similar to today's Council Tax, and each tithing was entitled to attend the local more or assembly. (*See* Dumb Borsholder.)

THE LITTLE HOPPERS HOSPITAL: A HOSPITAL IN A PUB

Father Richard Wilson was a vicar in Stepney, and when almost all his congregation removed to Kent during the hop-picking season, he decided to go with them. In 1898 he gave over his rented cottage at Five Oaks Green to be used as a hospital, where the sick children of hop pickers were cared for by three volunteer nurses. By 1910, the tiny hospital was overflowing, and the Revd Wilson bought the Rose and Crown pub, which was converted into a hospital with twelve wards, catering for both women and children. The Mission, as it came to be known, held services every Sunday.

Hoppers in this and other areas were also visited by members of the Salvation Army, who dispensed medical aid and religious advice along with hot food and the opportunity for a bath.

LOOKERS' HUTS: SHEPHERDS' HOMES

The Black Death brought about a huge change in the landscape of Kent. Romney Marsh had long been used for sheep farming, with the hardy Romney sheep able to survive well on the salt marshes, but after the plague, swathes of land lay untended and absentee landlords bought up the land and populated it with sheep, employing independent shepherds to look after them.

These 'lookers' might have half a dozen flocks to care for and during lambing season they lived out in the 'lookers' huts' that can still be seen in the area. There were once perhaps 350 of these tiny one-roomed cottages on the marsh, each made of brick with Kent peg tiles on the roof, but today there is barely a handful, each one standing forlorn on the windswept marsh. One window and a fireplace to warm your dinner and any motherless lambs were all that was needed, and although they were basic, they provided shelter from the elements for a man and his dog.

A newspaper article of 1904 reports that a looker was paid one shilling and sixpence per acre, per annum, which seems very little, considering it was a year-round job, including lambing and shearing as well as feeding and doctoring the sheep. However, when farms could be as large as 600 acres each, the sums earnt were not inconsiderable.

A looker's hut.

LOST ISLANDS: GONE BUT NOT FORGOTTEN

Kent's coast was once surrounded by islands; in the eighth century, Nennius tells us, there were 340 separate islands in what is now Romney Marsh alone, now mostly absorbed into the mainland by natural silting up as well as man-made reclamation.

Sheppey

On the Isle of Sheppey (the Sheep Isle), Harty and Elmley were once separate islands. Elmley once had a church, a farmhouse, a few houses, about 6,000 sheep, and was separated from Sheppey by a waterway known as The Dray.

Thanet

The Isle of Thanet was once divided from the mainland by the Wantsum Channel, over 2 miles wide at some points. Shipping charted a route through this channel to avoid going around the dangerous headland at the mouth of the River Thames.

Oxney

The Isles of Oxney and Ebony, near Appledore, are now 10 miles inland, but in the seventeenth century were only accessible by boat. Nearby Lydd was built on what was, at that time, a separate island. A combination of long-shore drift, changes to the Rother River's course, and 'inning' or reclaiming the land have joined this area to the mainland.

M

MADDER DYED SILK: PINK PERFECTION WITH A SECRET INGREDIENT

The town of Crayford, located between Bexley and Dartford, but not in the Borough of Bexley, was once famous for its high-quality pink silk, made by David Evans and Co.

The company was set up in the mid-nineteenth century as a silk retailer, but soon moved into dyed silk, specialising in madder dyed silk and hand block printing, a process it continued until the 1980s. The silk was luxurious, exclusive, and worn only by those rich enough to be able to afford it. They may not have been so keen, however, if they had looked a little more closely into the production process.

The nearby River Cray provided water, and the factory was situated near the purpose-built cattle sheds, which provided a constant supply of a secret ingredient that was used in the dying process. Nobody knows for sure what that mystery ingredient was, but we can all make a very good guess!

MAGICAL MYSTERY TOUR: THE BUS LEAVES FROM WEST MALLING AIRFIELD

The Beatles visited Kent in 1967 to film their short film, *The Magical Mystery Tour*, using the decommissioned RAF airfield at West Malling as the main location. Sharp-eyed viewers will also recognise the Town News newsagents in West Malling's High Street as the shop from which Ringo buys his tickets.

THE MAGNA CARTA: A LIMIT ON THE POWER OF THE KING

King Richard I was followed by his brother John, whose name is stamped indelibly on the memory as the signatory on the Magna Carta. Although born in Lincolnshire, Stephen Langton was appointed as Archbishop of Canterbury in 1206 and became a Man of Kent. The charter was signed on 15 June 1215, and it is an almost forgotten fact that Stephen Langton played an important role in the genesis of the paper, which was intended to limit the power of the monarch. In fact, the final Magna Carta was not signed and approved until 1225, after many updates and threats from the Church, the noblemen and the king. In the end, Stephen Langton issued a proclamation that anyone who went against the Magna Carta would be excommunicated, a fate almost worse than death in medieval England, and this smoothed the way to a balance of power between the king and Parliament.

MARC CHAGALL AND THE STAINED GLASS OF TUDELEY: FINE ART IN THE LOCAL COMMUNITY

The unusual stained-glass windows of All Saints' Church in Tudeley, located between Tonbridge and Paddock Wood, are beautiful, but they are also important because they were designed by Russian artist Marc Chagall. The only other stained glass in the UK by Chagall is in Chichester.

The first window at Tudeley was commissioned by the parents of Sarah d'Avigdor-Goldsmid, who died in a sailing accident aged just 21, but when Chagall arrived at the church in 1967 for the dedication he offered to create designs for the remaining eleven windows. The existing Victorian stained-glass windows were removed and are now on show in the vestry. All Saints is the only church in the world to have all twelve windows designed by Chagall, which were finally installed in 1985.

Those readers interested in stained glass may like to know that the oldest stained glass in the country is also in Kent, in St Mary's church, Brabourne.

MARY CARLETON: CON-ARTISTE EXTRAORDINAIRE

Mary Moders was born in Canterbury in 1642 to a modest tradesman. Such humble beginnings gave no indication of the huge notoriety the woman would command before her death and she was hanged thirty years later at Tyburn, a small village on the outskirts of London

Mary was married young, and bore two children. Both died, and when no more were born, Mary left Canterbury and began the life of a trickster, luring men into bigamous marriage with her and then leaving with a large part of their wealth. When the bigamy to her second husband was discovered, she quickly left the country and lived in Cologne for a while before returning to England, still only 21, with a whole new persona – she had suddenly become a German princess, albeit living on the stolen wealth of a German nobleman. Her third husband was John Carleton, whose name she kept until her death, despite several liaisons in between.

Mary's life was an incredible series of adventures and triumphs, and she herself capitalised on this by putting her acting skills to good use in a play about her life. She also wrote several pamphlets and was known to be not only beautiful but also witty.

Mary was transported to Jamaica in 1470, after she was found guilty of stealing a silver tankard, but, amazingly, she returned two years later and was arrested for returning from penal servitude without permission. It was for this crime that she was sentenced to death and hanged in 1473.

MIRACLE AT ST EUSTACE'S WELL: DEMONIC BLACK TOADS VANQUISHED BY THE WATERS

The Well at Withersdane near Wye was blessed by St Eustace, Abbot of Flai, in the thirteenth century and was considered to be holy from that day forward.

Its miraculous properties were confirmed when a woman suffering from dropsy drank of the waters, and vomited. Up came two black toads, which, to the amazement of the onlookers, changed into dogs and then asses. Quickly, water from the well was sprinkled between the woman and the animals, to break the bond, and they vanished into thin air.

The well is now on private property, but is still considered to provide healing relief from eye infections.

MOHINDER SINGH PUJJI: AN INDIAN PILOT IN THE RAF

Mohinder Singh Pujji was one of twenty-four Indian pilots to fly for the RAF during the Second World War, and it is his image that has been used in the memorial statue in Gravesend.

Squadron Leader Pujji was seconded from the 25,000-strong Indian Air Force during the Second World War, joining the thirteen Indian pilots already in the RAF, and was among the pilots from India who distinguished themselves in battle.

The bronze statue was erected in 2014 and bears the inscription: 'To commemorate those from around the world who served alongside Britain in all conflicts 1914–2014.'

Sqn Ldr Pujji stayed in the UK after the war and is buried in Gravesend.

THE MONTGOMERY MERMAID: A STARK REMINDER OF SOMETHING SINISTER

The Montgomery Mermaid is a bizarre piece of public art by Marvellous Murals, featuring the motto 'Welcome to Sheerness, You'll have a Blast'. Although confusing to visitors, locals recognise this as a reference to the Second World War ammunition ship SS *Richard Montgomery*, which lies only half-submerged off the coast of Sheppey. Although partially emptied soon after it foundered, the ship still contains an estimated 1,400 tonnes of explosives that are too unstable for reclamation to be attempted. Some experts contend that the boat could explode at any time, potentially flattening the land for 10 miles around and causing a tsunami wave of up to 40ft high to roll over Sheppey and up the Thames.

The ship is surveyed regularly by laser and multi-beam sonar and an equal number of experts believe it to be relatively stable, as the water around the bombs will stop them all exploding at once. Are those who live within the blast range living on borrowed time, or safe as houses? Only time will tell.

THE MOOT HORNS OF KENT: ANOTHER LOST TRADITION

There are seven Moot Horns of Kent, each associated with a city or Borough Council, many of which were the original Cinque Port towns. They were originally used to call burghers to the moot, or council, meetings of the area, but are now used for purely ceremonial purposes, and in some cases for display only.

Faversham, Folkestone, Sandwich, Canterbury, New Romney, Hythe and Dover once all had horns, but sadly the Moot Horn of Dover was stolen in 1967.

It is interesting to note here that the name of the manor house Ightham Mote derives its name from the word 'moot' not the word 'moat', although it is surrounded by water.

MUDDIES: SALT OF THE EARTH

A muddie, or a skevalman, was a person who dug clay or mud from the River Medway and tossed it onto a waiting barge to be taken to the nearby cement works. Digging the heavy, wet clay was hard work, and to see a gang working in unison, some digging left-handed and some right-handed, would have been a sight indeed.

Workers waited until low tide, so the clay-rich mud was exposed, using narrow-bladed spades that allowed them to dig more easily. They loaded the mud onto the barge, which had settled in the mud nearby, running up a board and throwing the mud in. As the tide came in, the barge began to float and was sailed up the river to the cement works.

N

THE NAILBOURNE: A SEVEN-YEAR ITCH

The Nailbourne is a stream with local celebrity. Said to rise every seven years, it in fact comes to life whenever prolonged rain saturates the ground and swells the spring that fuels it. Running along the Elham Valley and on to the River Stour, the stream is a nuisance to farmers, but a delight to walkers and local historians. It is a little local peculiarity that is 'our stream'.

Legend has it that the stream was brought forth by St Augustine, who visited the valley during a drought and prayed for water. Thinking that a constant flow might be taken for granted by the local people, he asked God to release the waters only once every seven years, thus reminding them at regular intervals of His presence.

Two other such nailbourne or eylebourn streams are seen at Cheriton and Bearsted. Sometimes known as Woe Waters, the streams are said to rise as a harbinger of disaster, with the fact that the stream that runs through the Addington Valley rose before the Second World War, causing a flood, adding weight to the claim.

NAPOLEON III AND HIS COURT IN KENT: A GRACIOUS WELCOME FOR NAPOLEON'S NEPHEW

There is still some debate about Chislehurst and whether or not it falls into the county of Kent. It was definitely within Kent until 1934, when it was in Chislehurst and Sidcup before being further divided between the London boroughs of Bexley and Bromley in 1965, and it is now counted as part of Greater London.

His Imperial Majesty Napoleon III of France, nephew of Napoleon I, was the first French president, and it was he who reluctantly took his country into the Franco-Prussian War. In 1870, the Prussians captured him and he subsequently fled to England, choosing exile over imprisonment. Napoleon and his family lived at Camden Place (now a golf club) but he died just three years after moving into the house, having been in poor health for many years. His wife and son stayed there until 1882, when, on the death of her son, Empress Eugenie moved away.

The family brought prosperity to the area, through their own expenditure and that of their guests, including the widowed Queen Victoria, but their short stay in our county is now all but forgotten.

NEW ROMNEY LOSES ITS STATUS: THE CHANGING OF THE RIVER ROTHER

Kent's coastline has never been stable, but one of the most spectacular changes came in 1287, when a great storm hit the eastern coast of England, following almost half a century of bad weather.

The Great Flood of 1287 was talked about in the years that followed much as we talk of the Great Storm of 1987, as the coastal surge caused terrific damage, even to inland areas.

The coastline of southern Kent was completely altered, creating new areas of land, changing the course of rivers and leaving ports stranded far inland. The River Rother was diverted away from the Kent port of New Romney to Rye, 15 miles away in East Sussex, taking away the livelihoods of the inhabitants overnight.

At St Nicholas' Church in New Romney, 4ft of silt built up inside the church, which now sits lower than the surrounding land and is to be found more than a mile inland; an astute visitor will be able to find a mooring ring in front of the church where boats once tied up. The towns on the north coast were also badly hit, with boats bring driven far inland across the flat wetlands.

NICHOLAS WOOD: THE GREAT EATER OF KENT

Nicholas Wood was born in Hollingbourne and soon moved to Harrietsham, where he became a local celebrity as a competition eater, taking on bets such as that with Sir Warham St Leger of Leeds Castle that he could eat a dinner intended for eight guests. He won the bet easily.

On another occasion, Wood is said to have eaten a whole sheep, and followed it up by three pecks of damsons (a peck is a tub large enough to hold 2 gallons).

Writing in 1630, John Taylor expounds Wood's virtues. The reason for his enthusiasm is that he was trying to generate interest in Wood, hoping to act as his agent in London, in which he saw the potential for huge profits.

Taylor recalls that Wood once ate enough for thirty men, after which servants rubbed his stomach with grease to allow the skin to expand enough to hold it all, and he also supposedly ate sixty eggs and 18 yards of black pudding.

Wood almost met an untimely end when John Dale of Lenham bet 2*s* that he could beat Wood's appetite. He presented Wood with twelve loaves of bread, soaked in beer, before a meal of roast beef. Wood consumed the bread but fell into an intoxicated stupor, not regaining consciousness for nine hours. This was one of the few bets he lost.

Taylor's pamphlet is full of praise for Wood and his eating exploits, saying that 'his guts are the Rendez-vous or meeting place … for the Beasts of the fields, the Fowles of the Ayre, and Fishes of the Sea'.

Wood never did join Taylor in London to make his fortune, and records do not show his fate. Perhaps he lived a long and happy life, or perhaps he died an early death through overeating. We will probably never know.

NOBODY'S FRIENDS: THE SECRET SOCIETY THAT STILL EXISTS

Although born in London, William Stevens had a sister who lived in Kent, and he was educated at Maidstone. Despite humble beginnings, he grew up to be a successful businessman but he never married. He was an unassuming man, and wrote prolifically under the pen name Nobody, a term equivalent to the more modern 'Everyman', believing he was of no more or less value than any other member of society.

In 1800, Stevens created the Society of Nobody's Friends. This was a group of fifty like-minded individuals who met just a few times a year to do good works, and who preferred to keep their identity private. The Society still exists, still keeps its membership to fifty, and still toasts the health of Nobody at every meeting.

NORTHBOURNE KNIFE CRIME: THERE ARE TWO SIDES TO EVERY TALE

The *Kentish Chronicle* of 30 July 1864 gives details of a crime that is still all too familiar: Stephen Jordan was accused of murdering George Church and wounding John Bushell and Stephen Amos.

John Bushell explained that he and several other men had left The Crown pub at Northbourne at about 11 p.m. and were overtaken in a laneway by Stephen Jordan, who picked a fight with them. George Church had told Jordan he was in no mood for a fight and was quite happy standing there holding up the finger post (*see* Bishop's Finger). Jordan returned to the pub but the men followed, and he attacked them with a knife, stabbing George Church in the side.

Evidence from the Superintendent at Sandwich shows that although Jordan did have a bloodstained knife, he was in fact sober and said, 'I did it in my own defence because they said they would murder or rob me.'

George Church did not die immediately, but passed away later from his wounds, and insisted that he and his friends had been innocent. Was this the case, or had the men waited for Jordan, who had fled back to the pub for safety, only to find he had been followed there by the mob?

One wonders if the alleged victims were known to the court, as the Judge, Mr Addison, said that in his opinion Jordan had acted in self-defence. Despite this, he was sentenced to eight months' hard labour.

OAK APPLE DAY: OR RESTORATION DAY

Oak Apple Day, falling on 29 May, Charles II's birthday, was not only a Kentish celebration, but a national holiday, to allow people to celebrate the restoration of the monarchy in 1660, after the eleven years of Commonwealth rule, when the country was without a king or queen.

The use of the oak as a symbol was a reference to the legend that King Charles hid in an oak tree to avoid capture, and this caught the imagination of the people. The custom of wearing oak leaves tucked into a waistband or hat persisted until the nineteenth century.

One of the biggest celebrations on this day was the Wye Races held in Fanscombe Valley on what the locals called Oak-Leaf Day.

OAST HOUSES: ICONIC SYMBOLS OF THE KENTISH COUNTRYSIDE

The iconic oast house is synonymous with the Kent countryside, although not exclusive to the county. The word itself comes from the Dutch word *eest*, meaning a drying kiln, and oasts were once used for drying lime as well as (later) hops.

Hops have been used in Britain since at least the ninth century, and are now an integral part of the beer-making process. However, when they were first introduced, they were used as packing material or animal fodder before they were considered suitable as a foodstuff for humans.

A field of hops is called a hop garden, and they once extended over much of Kent, making the county wealthy. Today, there are only about 1,000 hectares under cultivation. The hop vine is actually a 'bine', and is known as such locally,

An oast house and hop garden.

the difference being that a vine climbs up its support by using tendrils and a bine climbs by wrapping its own shoots around the support, using spiny hairs along the length to help it grip.

The drying houses have always been called oast houses, but the conical design was only introduced in the nineteenth century, and they quickly took over from the previous rectangular design. A fire is lit in the lower part of the conical section and the hops are placed on a slatted floor above. The shape means that air is drawn up through the building and the white cowl on the top is turned to catch the wind by the protruding tongue on front. Once the hops are dry, they are moved to another part of the oast house to cool.

ODIN AND THE SHEEP: A VIKING PRACTICE IN THANET

The Vikings settled briefly in Thanet in the ninth century, and yet in 1893, the echoes still rippled across the landscape.

T.W.E. Higgens, writing in 1896, reported that he himself had seen the bones of a sheep hanging in a tree near Westbere and asked the reason of a local shepherd. He was amazed to hear that several sheep had died, and that the local response was to hang one of the carcasses in a tree.

Higgens saw in this the remnants of the worship of Odin, Norse god of wisdom and war, and has attributed the custom to Viking beliefs that have never been discarded. I, for one, am tempted to believe him.

OPERATION DUKE: THE STRUGGLE TO FIND APRIL'S KILLER

Kent Police never close an unsolved case, even though the chances of finding the culprit are sometimes slim to non-existent.

One case they have never been able to solve is the infanticide of a newborn baby in Ashford in 1995. The tiny child had been suffocated, wrapped in a plastic bag and thrown into Singleton Lake. The body was found soon after it was dumped, and investigating officers gave her the name April, from the month she was found. Despite their best efforts, they were never able to find either the mother or the killer.

April was laid to rest in the Bybrook Cemetery in Kennington, Ashford, until 2011, when advanced in DNA technology made it possible to collect critical information from the body. The child was exhumed and re-examined, before she was reinterred after a short ceremony.

Despite the DNA, April's parents have never been found. She lies in her quiet grave, tended by local people, who still lay toys and flowers for her, dependent on the kindness of strangers.

OPERATION FORTITUDE: A LESSON IN MISDIRECTION

Towards the end of the Second World War, as the Allies prepared to invade France, it looked like southern Kent was a hotbed of activity, full of soldiers and armaments, preparing to attack the enemy.

Devised in preparation for the Normandy landings during the Second World War, Operation *Fortitude* was divided into two parts; Operation *Fortitude North* purported to be the preparations for an invasion of Norway and Operation *Fortitude South*, centred on Dover, was an elaborate ruse to convince the German army that Britain was going to invade at the Pas-de-Calais, which was, after all, the shortest route across the English Channel. It was hoped that German troops would be drawn away from the real invasion site on the beaches of Normandy, which happened in June 1944.

A fictitious First US Army Group (FUSAG) was invented, which undertook the supposed construction of roads, bridges, buildings, airfields and embarkation points. As well as mock buildings, dummy aircraft, tanks (either wooden or inflatable) and landing crafts were created, and false radio transmissions were made.

The deception worked, and Hitler moved troops to the Calais region. In fact, he was so convinced that an attack would come from Dover that the majority of troops remained in place until the end of July.

THE OSSUARY AT ST LEONARDS, HYTHE: A GRISLY REMINDER THAT DEATH IS ALL AROUND US

The ossuary at St Leonard's church in Hythe is, as the name suggests, a collection of bones, and, although they exist elsewhere in the country, it is a rare thing to find one open to the public. Thousands of skulls and other bones have been collected in the crypt of the church, and have been on display for at least 200 years, drawing visitors from all over the country.

It is estimated that the bones are the remains of up to 4,000 people, but where they came from or why they are there remains a mystery. The church was built over 1,000 years ago, so it is possible that the bones are at least that old, if not older. It has never been conclusively established whether they are the remains taken from a battlefield, a reused churchyard, or even a plague pit, or whether they have been collected from elsewhere. It is even more astounding to think about the people who gathered the bones, carefully built the custom-made shelving for the skulls and maintained the collection over the years. Each of these tantalising conclusions has its flaws, and until exhaustive scientific tests are carried out, the origin of the bones remains unknown.

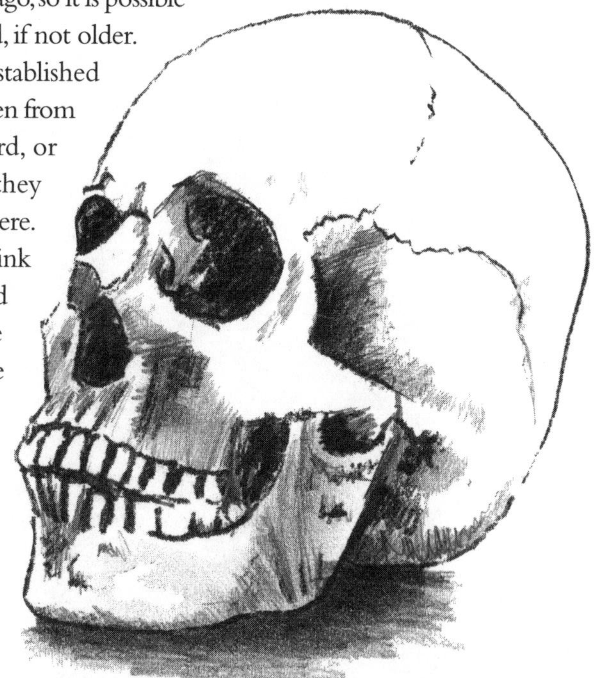

OXO: GOOD HEALTH FOR A PENNY

One of the most iconic brands of British industry was born here in Kent, in the tiny village of Hawkhurst.

Charles Gunther was born in America to German parents, and moved to Hawkhurst, near Tunbridge Wells, with his family when he was 40, buying the impressive Tongswood Estate, which he vastly improved, using local labour.

Gunther was chairman of the German company Liebigs, which already produced Extract of Beef, a product championed by Florence Nightingale, among others, as a meat substitute. Gunther was keen to reduce the cost to the man in the street, and after he oversaw the introduction of the product in liquid form, was keen to keep going. His aim was to create a product that could be sold for one penny to the general population, and after many trials, in 1910 he did just that.

As the war with Germany threatened, Gunther stood down as chairman and the company was renamed. Bricks on the front of the manor house, now used as a school, make the letters OXO, which was adopted as the new name of the company, but whether the lettering or the name came first is anyone's guess.

PADDLESWORTH: A LITTLE VILLAGE WITH A BIG HEART

The little village of Paddlesworth has fewer than fifty inhabitants, and yet it is one of the most visited places in the area.

Located on one of the highest points in the landscape, the village was used in the 1780s as one of the points of reference between Paris and the Greenwich Observatory.

The early Norman church is a magnet for those looking for charm and genuine antiquity, and is complemented by the nearby Cat and Custard Pot pub, which was used by fighter pilots in the Second World War.

Despite its many attractions, Paddlesworth is naturally self-deprecating, and the village motto is 'Highest Church, Lowest Steeple, Poorest Parish, Fewest People'.

PALM TREES AND PUSSY WILLOW: A TREE CAN BE WHATEVER YOU WANT IT TO BE

The Christian calendar includes the festival of Palm Sunday, which falls a week before Easter, and churches across the country look for palmate leaves to represent the palm fronds that welcomed Jesus into Jerusalem.

Worshippers in east Kent once used the branches of a tree that was almost always planted near a church: the yew. Churches were often encircled with five or six yew trees, and the branches were used in the annual Palm Sunday service; the tree came to be known locally as the palm tree.

Some churches in the Weald of Kent also used branches from the willow tree, as the white, furry buds that give it the name 'pussy willow' come out in the springtime. The variety used is known locally as the Pussy Palm or Palm Sallow.

The practice was once reflected in the names of public houses – there was a Palm Tree Inn at Wigmore and at Woodnesborough – but now only exists in road names, such as Palm Tree Lane at Adisham.

PANTILES: PAID FOR BY QUEEN ANNE

Before Queen Anne took the throne, she delighted in visiting, and in 1698 she took a trip to Tunbridge Wells. Her son, then the Duke of Gloucester, fell over while playing near the shops and Queen Anne donated £100 to the town for the installation of a tiled walkway.

The town council took the money, but were slow in laying the paved area, and when Anne returned the next year, she was vexed to see that it had not been completed, leaving immediately.

The tiles did eventually go down, and although they have now been replaced by modern paving, the area is still called 'The Pantiles'.

PAYING THE FOOTING: A HOP-FIELD TAX

The country practice of exacting a fee from a newcomer found its way into the hop fields of Kent when hoppers from London came in their thousands to work in the fields.

Any person who had not visited before had his shoes wiped with an apron or hop-bine and was required to 'pay his footing'. Any gentleman who refused to pay was pushed into the nearest hop bin to bring him to his senses.

This seems to be a derivation of the more established practice in other parts of the country, and I would suggest that only the younger gentlemen were treated in this way, amongst much hilarity from the young female hoppers.

PENENDEN HEATH: PLACE OF EXECUTION

Long known as the place for large public meetings, Penenden Heath, near Maidstone, was the location of Kent public hangings until in 1831 they moved to the roof of Maidstone gaol. It had taken the residents of Penenden thirty years of petitioning to persuade the authorities to move the proceedings, concerned not so much with the gruesome aspect of the spectacle, but with the amount of damage caused to their properties by the spectators. Hangings were carried out in public until 1868, when the practice was abolished.

The first executions on Penenden Heath were a simple undertaking, with the condemned man or woman being 'turned off' from the back of a cart, which was not always fatal. The trapdoor was introduced in the 1820s, and was more effective.

The last man to be hanged at Penenden was 19-year-old John Dyke, who was accused of burning a hay rick and was hanged in 1830. He was buried at Bearsted and his grave was initially marked with a Canadian cypress tree, which was taken down in 1996, but a plaque still marks the spot. Sadly, another man later confessed to the crime, and although buried in the same churchyard, was placed well away from the grave of John Dyke.

THE PILGRIMS WAY: THE ROAD TO REDEMPTION

When humans first came to England, crossing from the continent into Kent, they started to explore routes north and south. They kept to the higher, chalky routes along the North and South Downs, keeping their feet relatively dry.

Later, after the murder of Thomas Becket, pilgrims used the same route when travelling from Winchester to Canterbury. Surprisingly, the exact route of the original Way is not known, despite its fame from works such as Chaucer's *The Canterbury Tales*. Many years of road-building, detours and rights-of-way have changed the route so many times, that the traveller cannot be sure they are stepping in the footsteps of the first pilgrims.

The route still travels along the North Downs and calls at many hostelries and hotels, but although we will never know the exact location of many of the stopping points and trackways, those travelling along the quiet stretches of the route can be sure to hear faint echoes of those who went before.

PIRATE JOHN WARD: A TRUE PRIVATEER AND ADVENTURER

After the threat of invasion by the Spanish Armada, many fishermen and sailors saw an opportunity to make some extra money plundering Spanish ships. Queen Elizabeth I recognised this practice as a legitimate enterprise and issued licences, called 'letters of marque'.

One sailor who took full advantage of this was John Ward, who was born in Faversham and rose to fame as a Robin-Hood-like swashbuckling privateer raiding the vessels of Catholic countries while sparing those from Britain. When James I came to the throne and rescinded the licences, John continued to take Spanish ships, but being now outside the law he was considered to be a pirate. He worked in the waters around Britain and in the Mediterranean, inspiring ballads and stories as his fame grew. Towards the end of his life, he accepted the teachings of Islam and changed his name to Issouf Reis, dying at the age of 70 in Tunisia.

PLACENAME PRONUNCIATION: THE VAGARIES OF THE KENTISH DIALECT

Kent has a distinctive dialect, laid down over millennia, and has roots in several languages. Kentish place names reflect the waves of different nationalities that have taken up residence in this, the Garden of England, and although many have become anglicised, many still retain vestiges of the old pronunciation.

Some of the more unusual ones are Wrotham (Rootham), Trottiscliffe (Trosley), Mongeham (Munje-um) and Mereworth (Merryworth). Some are mere contractions such as Twydall (Twiddle), Teston (Tesson), Shipbourne (Shibbun) and Teynham (Tenham). Names ending in 'ge' are pronounced as 'je' as in Denge (Denje) and Lyminge (Limminje), which is a reminder of our Jutish forebears.

Our Celtic roots are to be found in names that derived from geological features such as Cefn, which means a ridge and was incorporated into Chevening; Pen, which means hill (Penshurst); and Dur which, means water (Derwent and River Dour), and Saxon words such as 'heng' – meaning wood or copse – give us Betteshanger and Westernhanger.

The Romans left their mark on our language as well, in place names that incorporated the word 'wick'. In many other parts of the country, this came from a Scandinavian word, but Kent did not suffer from the Viking invasions as much as other places, and the word derives from the Latin *vicus*, a row of houses. The Normans, of course, brought with them the French language, which persists in names such as Wickhambreaux (Wickambroo), Capel-le-Ferne (Cay-pel) and Upper and Lower Hardres (Hards).

It is interesting to note that several words of Kentish dialect have made their way into place names. The words Forstal, Minnis and Lees all mean 'a common' and appear in place names across the county.

PLANTAGENET ROYALTY LIVING INCOGNITO: DID A PRINCE WALK AMONG US?

Interest in the Plantagenet dynasty has been revived since the discovery of the body of King Richard III in the car park in Leicester, and the county of Kent has a part to play in this history. It is said that, along with his one legitimate son, he also fathered three illegitimate children, one of whom was Richard of Eastwell, who lived in Kent from about 1540.

It is said that young Richard had been taken to Richard III just before the Battle of Boswell in 1485, and was told the truth of his parentage. After Richard III's death in that battle, young Richard fled to Kent and subsequently worked as a bricklayer for Sir Thomas Moyle in Eastwell, and sometime later revealed his secret to his employer. Sir Thomas believed him, and gave him a small house, on the site of the more modern Plantagenet Cottage, and an allowance.

When he died in 1515, 81-year-old Richard was buried in Eastwell church, which has now fallen into disrepair. However, the church records are still available and the entry for Richard's death reads 'Rychard Plantagenet was buryed the 22nd daye of December anno ut supra. Ex registro de Eastwell sub anno 1550.' It is annotated with the symbol that was by custom added to the entries of nobility, and would not normally be seen alongside the entry for an aged bricklayer, even if he had shown a the surprising ability to read book in Latin.

Further controversy comes to light when we consider the evidence given in David Baldwin's book *The Lost Prince*, which suggests that Richard was actually Richard of York, the younger of the Princes in the Tower, which adds a further layer of mystery to the story.

A tomb in the churchyard bears the inscription 'Reputed to be the grave of Richard Plantagenet', but despite calls for DNA testing of remains within the tomb, the fact is that we may never know the truth.

THE PLUM PUDDING RIOTS: NOBODY TAKES OUR CHRISTMAS!

In 1647 the Puritan government issued an edict that Christmas should not be celebrated and that shops should open as usual on 25 December, which fell on a Saturday. There were to be no garlands of greenery and certainly no 'plum pottage or nativity pies'. They believed that the overindulgence in food and alcohol and the gay abandon of carols, games and plays were sinful.

The citizens of Canterbury ignored the law and when the Mayor stepped in, threatening to arrest the shopkeepers who refused to open, he himself was thrown into gaol. The Royalists barred the gates to the city and proclaimed it a Royalist stronghold.

The rioting went on until the end of January, growing in size and intensity until 1,000 citizens were involved, fighting with muskets, clubs or their fists. Eventually, 3,000 Parliamentarian soldiers were sent in and the ringleaders were arrested. After several months in prison they were put on trial at Maidstone. Luckily, they were released, and there were wild celebrations in Canterbury.

PLUTO, DUMBO AND THE PWD: HELPING TO WIN THE WAR

The Pipeline Under the Ocean (PLUTO) was created during the Second World War by the PWD (Petroleum Warfare Department) and is said to have saved countless lives just by being there. Its purpose was to transport fuel from

England to the continent after D-Day, and it stretched from Dungeness to Boulogne, supported by miles of pipeline that connected it to refineries across the country.

PLUTO was a network of seventeen lines, lying on the bed of the English Channel, each joined to a pumping station (code named Dumbo) disguised as a holiday home at Dungeness, to hide it from enemy aerial reconnaissance. Emergency tanks were also in place along the beach, each cunningly disguised, to be used in case of interruption to the fuel supply. By the end of the war, almost two million gallons of fuel had been pumped across.

PUDDING PANS: ROMAN TREASURE FROM THE SEA

About 3 miles north of Herne Bay is the curiously named Pudding Pan Rock, lying near the sandbank known as Pan Sands. The rock has become famous in archaeological circles as the site of the wreck of a Roman ship.

The ship was carrying a cargo of red Samian tableware from central Gaul and although the ship itself has never been recovered, about 700 dishes and bowls are now held in museums across the UK. Dishes dredged up by the oyster fishermen or washed ashore were once coveted by the Whitstable housewife, to be used as a pudding pan, and many remain in private ownership.

A pudding pan, dredged up near Herne Bay.

A further mystery is revealed when we read the *Archaeologia* of 1779, in which there is an article by Thomas Pownall, who visited the site in 1773, and dredged up lumps of Roman concrete, brickwork and other rubble. He surmises that a Roman building had once existed on the sands, which had at that time been one of several islands in the Thames Estuary. He suggests that the building was built specifically for the manufacture of Samian ware, although it is more likely to have been the site of a Roman lighthouse, and that a cargo ship foundered on the rocks during a storm.

Perhaps modern technology will reveal more secrets of the Roman pudding pans, but for now their story remains hidden.

PUDDING PIES AND CHERRY BRANDY: AN EASTER TREAT

A particularly Kentish speciality is the Pudding Pie, a tart made from eggs, rice, currants and lemon, that can be eaten at any time of year, but especially on Ash Wednesday. It was created to use up all the kitchen ingredients that are not allowed during Lent. An alternative name for the treat is the Kent Lent Tart.

Brand's *Popular Antiquities* of 1905 describes the Kentish custom of 'pudding-pieing'. After the privations of Lent, it was the custom, for young people especially, to travel from pub to pub, eating small pudding pies and drinking cherry brandy.

PRISONER OF WAR CAMPS: KEEP YOUR ENEMIES CLOSE

Being the main port of entry into the UK, Kent was the place chosen for many prisoner-of-war camps, as armies were keen to dispose of their charges as soon as they could. One such place is Sissinghurst Castle, which was leased by the government in 1756 to house French seamen captured in the Nine Years' War.

Up to 2,000 men were kept in cramped conditions and riots were not unusual. The building was all but stripped by men seeking an exit or just looking for firewood. Luckily for the owners, they were paid compensation when the war ended seven years later, although it was not enough for a full refurbishment, and the house gradually fell into disrepair. Today, only the gatehouse remains.

Things looked bleak for the castle until the 1930s, when a descendant of the family who built the castle in 1573 bought the land and buildings and began restoration. Vita Sackville-West and her husband Harold Nicolson worked tirelessly on the house and gardens, and the rest, as they say, is history.

By the end of the seventeenth century, it was deemed safer to house prisoners offshore and old ships, at the end of their useful life, were used to house prisoners. Soldiers from the Napoleonic Wars were kept on hulks moored in the River Medway and the River Thames, each housing an average of 1,000 men in a space deemed suitable for 400. Conditions were bleak and many men took advantage of the skills of local fishermen who were willing to help them to escape, all paid for by the relatives of the man in question. (*See* Deadman's Island.)

Escapees made their own way from the Medway towns to London, where they were easily picked up by Whitstable hoys, fishing boats or oyster boats to be dropped off at Seasalter. The men then made their way across country, stopping at predetermined safe-houses and were collected at Swalecliffe for the crossing to Flushing, Dunkirk or Ostend.

PRIMOGENE DUVARD: WRITER OF RELIGIOUS TEXTS

Primogene Duvard was born at Borden, near Sittingbourne, in 1823, and lived with her mother. Primogene became known for her religious and historical poems, plays and devotional writings, particularly her play about Mary Tudor.

Sadly, the *London Daily News* of 2 December 1847 carried the following text:

> Dated this day of December, 1847 MRS. DUVARD and her DAUGHTER, Primogene Duvard, authoress of several publications, having become, through a variety of circumstances over which they had no control, reduced to a state of the utmost distress, SOLICIT the AID of their friends to relieve their present difficulties, and enable them, to recommence business for themselves in future. Mrs. Duvard has during a period of 10 weeks suffered severely from sciatica and acute rheumatism, which threaten to disable her through the winter, as she is somewhat advanced in life and afflicted with other serious complaints; and Miss Duvard's health will not admit of her obtaining a livelihood entirely by her own exertions during the illness of her mother. Any contributions addressed to Mrs. DUVARD, Borden. Sittingbourne, Kent, will be promptly and gratefully acknowledged.

Four years later, in the 1851 census, Primogene's occupation is given as 'authoress', but it was obviously an occupation that did not pay well enough.

Mrs Duvard lived on until 1861, aged 72, and Primogene died at Pond Farm, Borden in 1877, aged just 54.

QUEEN OF THE DESERT: FOLLOWED HER DREAMS

Lady Hester Stanhope held court as Queen of the Desert, but died in poverty and obscurity.

Lady Hester was born in Chevening to eccentric parents, and soon followed them into a world of pleasure and fantasy, maintaining an easy dominance over her acquaintances by virtue of her wit and good nature.

In 1803 she moved to Walmer Castle to live with her uncle William Pitt the Younger, becoming the de facto First Lady. He spoilt his favourite niece and she rewarded him by nursing him until his death in 1806.

By 1810 she was bored with England, and travelled to Gibraltar and thence to the Middle East, settling in Lebanon, where she bought a castle and transformed herself into the Queen of the Desert, adopting a lavish lifestyle.

She continued to be dictatorial and yet with a warm heart, offering a refuge to the sick and homeless and receiving regular visits from her old friends from England. Her habit of wearing men's trousers, waistcoat and even a turban scandalised and titillated the visitors. Sadly, she became more and more reclusive as she grew older, and in 1838 shut herself away from the outside world entirely. She died in poverty the following year and was buried in her own garden.

QUEEN OF THE HOPS: WHITBREAD'S HOP FESTIVAL

Every industry likes to celebrate its achievements and many have their own annual festival with a queen of the industry, be it a coal queen or a glass queen, and her court presides over the celebrations. In 1948, the Whitbread Hop Farm at Beltring celebrated its first hop festival, which grew in popularity over the years. Even though fewer hands were needed to pick the hops, numbers at the festival increased until they reached 3,000 at their peak, consisting of families who wanted to revisit their happy times in a hopper's hut, as well as those currently working.

As with all industries, mechanisation gradually took over, manpower was reduced and few people attended the festival. In 1968 the event was devastated by a flash flood and this became the final nail in the coffin of a failing venture. It was the last hop festival held on the site.

THE QUEENBOROUGH TORNADO: FANTASTIC PHENOMENON OR FANTASTICAL FIB?

The railway brought great prosperity to southern England, as passengers travelled through the county to reach the continent. The early days, however, were filled with tales of death and disaster. Even Charles Dickens suffered minor injuries in a train crash on the railways of Kent.

The early months of 1876 have gone on record as being particularly cold, with blizzards in parts of the country. On 19 March, so *The Standard* reports, a gust of wind blew down a shed 180ft long, killing carpenter John Brown.

Despite the weather, he was engaged in the construction of the London, Chatham and Dover Railway pier, which being built for the convenience of passengers travelling by steam boat to and from Flushing, in the Netherlands. When the coroner asked why the shed should have blown down, when only the frame had been completed and the wind should have passed right through it, a witness reported that it had been a whirlwind, which suddenly blew in and just as suddenly abated. With no further evidence, a verdict of accidental death was returned.

Is it possible that a whirlwind came from nowhere and blew down a 180ft shed? The jury did not dispute the fact. If I were in Queenborough on a blustery March day, I would be wary, just in case. Wouldn't you?

THE QUENINGATE: FIT FOR A QUEEN

The name Queningate is a contraction of the words Queen's Gate, and it was this Roman gate through the city walls that enabled Queen Bertha, wife of King Ethelbert, to walk from the grounds of the Cathedral to St Martin's

Queen Bertha and her husband, King Ethelbert of Kent.

church. The current Queningate in Canterbury leads from the precincts of Canterbury Cathedral out onto the ring road that encircles the city, but the original gate was situated much further to the right, now in the corner of the car park.

It is said that it was Queen Bertha who encouraged Ethelbert to adopt Christianity, which paved the way for the visit of St Augustine. St Martin's church was built during the Roman occupation and it has been in continuous use as a place of worship ever since.

Both King Ethelbert and Queen Bertha have statues to their memory on Lady Wooton's Green in Canterbury.

QUINTAIN: PREPARATION FOR WAR

The only remaining quintain in England is on the village green at Offham. Erected during the reign of Elizabeth I, it was used for jousting practice, and although the current post may have had parts replaced over the years, it is a unique survival from the days of jousting.

The quintain was a training device, used in the sport of 'tilting', or practising for the joust. It is described by John Britton as:

> an upright post of wood fixed in the ground, with the upper part rounded so as to receive the socket of a cross-piece, one end of which is expanded like a fan, and pierced full of boles: to the other end is attached a bag of sand, which swung round with a force proportionate to the blow given to the broad part of the transverse, when the game of the Quintin was played.

A player rode at the quintain, aiming to hit a target suspended on a rotating arm, judging the speed needed for accuracy against that needed to get out of the way of the arm as it spun towards him. Given that the arm would have been weighted, it probably came round at a fair speed.

The quintain post in Offham.

THE RATTLING CAT: AN EARLY EARLY-WARNING SYSTEM

In the heyday of smuggling activities, almost everyone was involved, from the housewife who pegged white washing on her line or swept her front step to signal the arrival of the Riding Officers to the pubs and inns that stored the contraband goods.

The Rattling Cat public house is now closed, but was once a popular destination on the outskirts of Deal, in the suburb of Walmer. Legend has it that the landlord was involved in 'the wicked trade', as smuggling was known, and that he kept several cats.

The cats played their part in his operations, having a selection of bones attached to their collars, which rattled as they walked. These rattling cats were apparently of use as an early warning system when the Excise Men approached, jangling their collars as they scurried for home.

THE RED DEAN: A COMMUNIST SYMPATHISER

Hewlett Johnson took the position of Dean of Canterbury Cathedral in 1931, and quickly became a local sensation. His teachings were those of love and forgiveness, but many of his beliefs came from the roots of Communism rather than from Christianity, and he called himself a Communist Christian.

Ignoring the darker side of Communist Russia, he toured the country, welcomed by Joseph Stalin, after which he visited Mao Tse Tung in China and, later, Fidel Castro. His teachings, along with his many books and pamphlets, split his congregation and earned him the nickname 'The Red Dean'. Despite censure from many parts of the Church, he was never removed from office, and served for over three decades. He was much admired throughout the city, particularly in the Second World War, during which he raised morale, gave aide, and sheltered the homeless.

Johnson died in 1966 at the age of 92, having completed his autobiography, *Searching for Light*.

THE RHEE WALL AND THE READING STREET SEWER: NEITHER A WALL NOR A SEWER

The Rhee Wall is a miracle of medieval engineering. It is a run of parallel banks enclosing a canal that travels over 7 miles from Appledore to New Romney, on the south coast of Kent. The word 'rhee' is an old English word for a watercourse, and its purpose was to channel water from inland Appledore out to the sea at Old Romney, clearing silt as it went, thus preserving the reclaimed land as a workable agricultural resource.

Despite the best efforts of the medieval engineers, the silt still built up and after 100 years the canal dried out and was no longer usable. Old Romney is now 4 miles inland and even New Romney, which replaced it, is now over a mile inland.

The New Salt Channel was created as an early effort to keep the waterway open, taking water from the River Rother northwards into the Kentish countryside. However, it quickly gained the nickname of 'The Reading Steet Sewer', after a nearby village, and it too is no longer used.

RICHARD TREVITHICK: LYING IN A PAUPER'S GRAVE

It is hard to underestimate the importance of Richard Trevithick to the development of the whole of the industrialised world, and yet he died poor and alone a long way from home.

Born in Cornwall, Trevithick invented and pioneered the steam engine as a mechanism for powering locomotives, and can be seen as the father of the rail industry.

Sadly, his work did not bring him fame and fortune during his lifetime, and he died almost penniless in Dartford in 1833. In fact, he had so little money to his name that there was not even enough for a burial and he was buried in an unmarked pauper's grave in St Edmund's Burial Ground, Dartford.

ROBINSON CRUSOE: A KENTISH TALE?

What on earth could *Robinson Crusoe* have to do with Seasalter, that tiny village just to the west of Whitstable? Quite a lot, according to Wallace Harvey in his 1989 book, *Seasalter and the Mystery of Robinson Crusoe*.

The book provides compelling evidence that Daniel Defoe was very familiar with this part of the north coast of Kent, suggesting that he may even have had relatives in the area. Drawing on the knowledge that Defoe regularly used real places as a basis for his writing, Harvey has meticulously researched the coastline from the time and suggests that Robinson Crusoe was actually shipwrecked on the Columbine sandbank and came ashore at Seasalter. Details such as the post on which Crusoe carved notches, the description of an offshore wreck used as accommodation by seasonal workers, and that, before the building of the sea wall, parts of Whitstable were once an island at high tide, seem to confirm his theory.

Even people born and bred in Whitstable, long known for its association with W. Somerset Maugham, are unaware that it had another even earlier association with the world of English literature.

ROCHESTER BRIDGE IS FALLING DOWN: FUNDRAISING THE MEDIEVAL WAY

Rochester Bridge has been an essential route from Kent to London and beyond since the eleventh century, and from the original wooden structure to the current modern design, has always been in need of repair and maintenance.

Many charities have used the idea of selling or auctioning donated goods to generate funds, but the Archbishop of Canterbury really raised the bar when he published a notice in 1489 offering 'a remission from purgatory for forty days, for all manner of sin' for anyone who donated to the cause. I wonder how many people took advantage of this most excellent offer to release their soul from torment.

ROYAL BRITISH LEGION INDUSTRIES: CARE FOR BRITISH SOLDIERS IN THE HEART OF OUR COUNTY

There are many charities that support ex-servicemen, but none are as well-known as the Royal British Legion. In operation since 1921, the charity gained its 'Royal' prefix in 1972 and is synonymous with its annual poppy appeal, raising funds to support servicemen and women in need.

The charity that is less well-known is the Legion's sister charity, Royal British Legion Industries. Set up in 1919 as Industrial Settlements Inc., for disabled ex-servicemen, the charity soon moved into Preston Hall in Aylesford, providing support for the thousands of wounded servicemen who had come home sick and injured from the First World War, in particular the 55,000 men suffering from tuberculosis. One of the men who benefitted from the specialist nursing was a young Eric Blair, who later wrote under the pen name George Orwell, who was admitted in 1938 after serving in Burma. The charity expanded, and now manages a community housing estate of over 300 homes as the Royal British Legion Village for service personnel. The scheme is still expanding, with planning for care suites and a day care centre to care for the ageing population.

Kent has much to offer those who live or work here as well as those who visit, so it should come as no surprise that our county was chosen as the location for a community where we can give back to those who gave so much for us.

ROYAL MILITARY CANAL: A LAST-DITCH ATTEMPT TO STOP THE FRENCH

In 1804 the first spade-full of dirt was removed from the channel that was to become known as the Royal Military Canal.

The country feared an attack by their old foe Napoleon Bonaparte, and the canal was constructed between Folkestone and Hastings to cut off any potential invading army, in the unlikely event that they managed to get past the Royal Navy and the Martello Towers.

The plan included a row of cannon positioned along the canal at 400-yard intervals, supported by soldiers and supplies that could be moved along the associated Military Road, which was protected by the bank of earth created when the canal was dug out, and crossed by means of the wooden bridges that would be erected at intervals.

The canal runs for 28 miles, is 30ft wide, and is now recognised as an important tool in the irrigation of the marshes as well as being a haven for wildlife. Barges no longer travel along the canal, and although it is possible to walk or cycle along the entire length, it is safe to say that no invading French army has ever crossed the canal.

RUNAWAYS: SOMETIMES IT WAS THE ONLY OPTION

In the days before divorce and when bankruptcy was the undoing of a man, sometimes the only option was to run away from it all. If he did, the welfare of his wife and any children fell to the parish, so every effort was made to catch and return him.

The *Maidstone Journal* of 22 November 1791 carried an offer of a reward for the capture of three men: Richard Cheeseman, John Mace and Abraham Ashdown. The reward for Richard Cheeseman was 5 guineas, and a single guinea for the other two men. This was equivalent to about £1,000 for John and Abraham and £5,000 for Richard.

Just ten years later, on 30 December 1801, things got too much for Richard Obee of Thurnham, and he absconded. A notice was duly put into the newspaper, giving him until 25 January to return, after which a warrant would be put out for his arrest. Richard was a bricklayer by trade, but seemed to be in debt, as the final line of the notice kindly advised him that 'his affairs were in a much better state than expected'. Perhaps there was light at the end of the tunnel, and I would dearly love to know if he returned home, was chased down by the law, or whether he escaped and set up a new life for himself elsewhere.

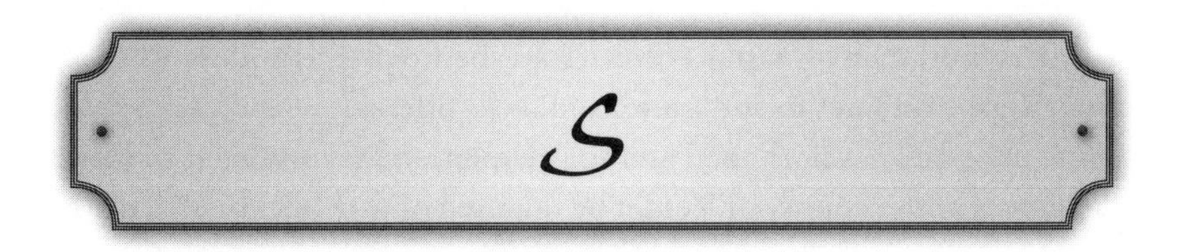

ST JOHN STONE: HANGED IN DANE JOHN GARDENS

Augustine Friar John Stone was one of the people who refused to accept that Henry VIII was the head of the Church, despite a very clear royal decree on the matter, known as the Act of Supremacy. He was kept in prison for a year, and then hanged, drawn and quartered in Dane John Gardens as an example to all. In 1970, he was canonised and became St John Stone. The friary to which he belonged has now long gone, and the area is now a shopping centre, but the name of that centre is Whitefriars, after the habits worn by the Augustinian Friars.

SALOMONS' SUCCESS: A SCIENTIST AND CAR ENTHUSIAST

Sir David Salomons estate at Southborough, near Tunbridge Wells, is well known as a tourist destination and wedding venue, but the true extent of the family's achievements are not so well understood. David was the first Jewish Lord Major of London, but died childless, passing his title to his nephew, David Lionel.

Sir David the Younger installed electricity throughout the whole house in 1882 and added a science theatre to the building. As well as pioneering scientific inventions, he was a keen collector of motor vehicles. He owned sixty-two different cars, and founded the Self-Propelled Traffic Association in 1895, which later became the Royal Automobile Club, or RAC. He was also the organiser of the first motor show in the country, in 1894. It was expected to be a small affair, held one Tuesday afternoon in October, with the expectation of a few hundred visitors. As it turned out, thousands arrived and a new phenomenon was born.

SAMPHIRE HOE: CREATED BY MAN BUT GIVEN TO NATURE

In a time when many coastal counties are bemoaning the loss of land to erosion, Kent continues to add more land to its title.

For many centuries both man and the elements have combined to increase the land mass in the county of Kent. The draining of marshland, particularly in the north-west and south-west of the county, has been happening for hundreds of years, and the number of lighthouses on Dungeness is testament to the continued movement of the shoreline.

The samphire plant, after which Samphire Hoe is named.

One new piece of land is barely twenty years old, and was created by man but given back to nature. The spoils of the Channel Tunnel excavations needed to go somewhere, and the base of the Shakespeare Cliff between Dover and Folkestone was ideal.

Opened in 1997, the 30-hectare site is now an award-winning nature reserve open to the public.

SEA FORTS: PROTECTION FROM THE ENEMY

Visitors to the north coast of Kent can look out into the estuary of the River Thames and see huge rusting buildings, balancing on spindly legs like advancing alien spiders. Once you get up close to them, though, their real character become clear.

The Grain Tower was built in the nineteenth century to counter the threat of an attack from our old enemy, France. The tower was a sister emplacement for the guns on the other side of the River Medway, on the island of Sheppey. The shifting sand and gravel proved a problem to the builders, and almost as soon as the three-storey building was completed in 1855 it was obsolete. It was eventually decommissioned in 1929 and is now in private hands.

Maunsell sea forts in the Thames Estuary.

The second set of sea forts visible from the coast around Whitstable and Herne Bay are the Maunsell Sea Forts, which were installed off the Kent coast in 1942 to counteract attacks from the Luftwaffe, who were using the Thames as a navigation aid on their way to bomb London. The three sets of forts – Shivering Sands, Red Sands and Nore – were built at Red Lion Wharf in Northfleet and floated down the river to be used as platforms for anti-aircraft guns. Each fort had seven towers, linked by walkways; there were initially 165 men in each tower, which was increased to 265 in 1944 to counter the V-1 flying bomb threat.

The forts were briefly used as a home for pirate radio stations in 1964–5, but have since been abandoned.

THE SEASALTER COMPANY: EXPLOITING LOOPHOLES IN THE LAW

The Seasalter Company operated between 1740 and 1854, working very close to, or even just over, the thin line between clever business practice and flouting the law.

The company was set up by a group of like-minded individuals to take advantage of the huge profits to be made from smuggling goods in and out of the country without paying either customs or excise tax. Those who rose to the higher positions in the company made huge profits and worked their way up the social ladder to become prominent members of their communities; one even became Mayor of Dover.

The operations were huge, and ranged from the north to the south coasts of Kent, employing hundreds of men. On one occasion, the Riding Officers reported that the loot landed by 150 smugglers on the north coast was carried away by over sixty men, using between eighty and ninety horses to carry the contraband. Goods were brought in by boat, and Joseph Collard, writing in 1902, describes a directional lantern, created with a funnel at the front, possibly several feet long, which could be used to locate landing points with as little visible light as possible.

Horses were kept ready on Seasalter Marshes, under the pretext of being put there for grazing, and goods were generally transported to Blue House Farm at Lenham before being dispatched to their final destination, hidden in carts with false bottoms and other such contrivances. Goods that could not be readily transported were hidden in the area, for example placed under haystacks, which could double in size overnight, before returning to their original size the next evening.

The men of The Seasalter Company were able to cross the marshy land by means of long planks, which enabled them to speed across the dykes and streams ahead of those in pursuit.

Although the men were well paid, it was the officials of the company who truly prospered. One of the ways in which they did this was through the buying and selling of property and land between themselves at inflated cost – what might today be called money laundering. The accounts of William Baldock, for example, show that on his death in 1812 his estate was worth over £1m, even though he had come from poor beginnings.

The company was run very successfully by what were generally considered to be respectable citizens, but eventually folded in 1854, as laws were tightened and smuggling became a less profitable enterprise.

SEAWEED FROM THE SHORELINE: A RICH BOUNTY FROM THE SEA

Looking down at the beaches of Thanet, many of which are stony and difficult to reach, it is hard to imagine that they were once important to both the farmer and the housewife in days gone by.

Samphire collected from the rocks on our southern coast was too valuable to be eaten by those who traded it to the big hotels and restaurants and they themselves would have eaten dulse or laver. Both have a high mineral content and were invaluable to those on a poor diet. People would also have collected sea kale, which is now a protected species.

Seaweed was also collected and used as animal feed in the winter or processed into kelp which was used as manure on the fields, or even as a fuel. Later, seaweed was broken down into its constituent chemical parts for use by the scientific community, for example iodine was used in the photographic industry.

THE SEVEN CHAMPIONS: A LIVING FOLK TRADITION IN THE WEST OF KENT

Kent is rather lacking in the tradition of mumming plays, which flourished in other parts of the country. It seems that the use of the Hooden Horse (*see* The Hooden Horse of East Kent) rendered an alternative means of entertainment redundant. However, the Hooden Horse was, in the main, associated with east Kent, and plays did develop in north and west Kent, particularly in the Darent Valley. One of these was the tale of the Seven Champions, and the men who performed were said to be 'championing'.

The characters varied from village to village and often appeared with blackened faces, to disguise the identity of the actor so they became more fully associated with the role they played, and they also disguised their figures with paper ribbons. Standard characters were St George (or King George), the Sweep, Father Christmas, Beelzebub, the Doctor, Slasher (or the Turkish Knight) and Jack, and the story centred around the slaying of Slasher by St George, who was then revived by the Doctor. Jack was the last character to appear, and would be the one to appeal to his hosts for donations; despite the light-hearted nature of the celebrations, the donations were a vital part of sustaining agricultural workers through the lean winter months.

Although almost exclusively seen in pubs and at festivals nowadays, the Champions once travelled around the county, calling at large houses in the way that carol singers do today, ending up in the heart of their own village.

THE SEVEN SISTERS: A SWEET CHESTNUT TREE LIKE NO OTHER

The sight of the Seven Sisters in Viceroy's Woods near Penshurst often stops visitors in their tracks, for the group is comprised of not one, not two, but seven trunks. The whole group measures over 5m in circumference and has enough room at its centre to accommodate up to a dozen people. Estimated to be over 30m high, the tree is possibly the largest living tree in Great Britain.

This amazing spectacle has formed around a rocky hillock in the middle, which has forced the branches to grow out around it. The tree is undoubtedly hundreds of years old, but the exact age has never been established. Likewise, the reason for the tree's unusual growth has never been fully understood. Some scientists have even suggested that the tree is actually a set of trees, planted together in one hole to create a folly or picnic spot for the local landowner.

Whatever the reason for its existence, the tree now stands in a public park where passers-by can sit quietly in its shade, look up through the rustling leaves and contemplate both the reason for the tree's existence and their own.

SHARP'S TOFFEE: A KENTISH SPECIALITY

Edward Sharp was born in Maidstone in 1854 and lived there until he died in 1931. His first business was a grocer's shop, which he ran in Week Street. In 1878 he began to sell home-made toffees, an enterprise that blossomed into an international business.

Ten years later, Sharp sold the grocer's shop and built a toffee factory in Sandling Road. Sharp's Toffee prospered and his flagship product, Kreemy Toffee, became so popular that in 1912 a new factory was built in St Peter's Street. Soon, Sharp's Toffee grew to be the biggest toffee manufacturer in the world, and Edward Sharp was granted a knighthood.

The company stayed in the family until 1961, but the post-war taste for chocolate had knocked Sharp's Super Kreem Toffee from the top of the sales chart, and Trebor bought the business. Sharp's toffees continued to roll off the production line until 1998, but the factory closed in 2000. The site was levelled and the plant has been replaced by housing.

The smell of the toffee factory still lingers in the memories of those who lived in Maidstone during its heyday, mingling with the unforgettable smell of the tannery, and many recall that those who worked there could eat the toffees as they worked, as long as they took none home.

THE SHEERNESS ECONOMICAL SOCIETY: THE OLDEST CO-OPERATIVE IN THE COUNTRY

Founded in 1816 to serve the dock workers on the Isle of Sheppey, the Sheerness Economical Society is the oldest co-operative society in Britain. The society, 'established by the officers and workmen of His Majesty's Dockyard, Ordnance and New Work at Sheerness' was established for the purpose of 'obtaining for themselves and their families, a supply of wheaten bread and flour and butchers meat' and was to be called the Economical Society.

Sheerness Dockyard.

In true co-operative fashion, the society bought at wholesale prices and passed the savings on to its members, initially selling from a cart going door-to-door. In 1850, the society bought its own shop, and went on to open dozens more across the Island. Eventually merging with the Co-operative Wholesale Society (CWS), the people of Sheerness have never forgotten that their society was the first of its kind.

SHELLS: A REMINDER OF OUR CLOSE LINKS WITH THE SEA

An air of mystery surrounds the Shell Grotto at Margate, from the first time you hear of its existence. Further research will tell you that not much is known about it at all, and that even estimates about its age are mere speculation.

The Grotto, as it is now called, was discovered in 1835 by Mr Newlove, a schoolteacher, when he was digging in the garden, in the oft-repeated tale of a small sinkhole opening up before him. Documentary evidence from Mr Newlove's daughter, however, insists that the she and her brother had already found the caves some time earlier, but kept it from their father, as their own particular secret.

An entrance was dug so that visitors could be welcomed, and it has remained almost as it was found for 180 years, with the addition of electric lighting to guide visitors down a steep passageway into the chamber within, which contains what looks very much like an altar. The surface of every wall and pillar and even the ceilings are covered with over four million shells, arranged in an array of intriguing patterns. Most of the shells are local, apart from the flat winkle, which is only found in the waters near Southampton, and as current academic opinion states that the caves date from the Bronze Age, this raises the question of how they came to be in Margate.

The church vestry of St James' church in Cooling is another shell-covered delight. Erected in the early nineteenth century, the decoration of the vestry may have taken inspiration from the Margate Shell Grotto. The walls are covered with thousands of cockleshells, possibly inspired by the fact that the scallop is the symbol of St James.

The church's other claim to fame is that it was allegedly the inspiration for Pip's graveyard in Charles Dickens' *Great Expectations*. As with all great stories, it is only partly true. There are thirteen children's graves in the churchyard, Charles Dickens did live nearby, and it is set in a desolate landscape. However, the graves belong to members of two different families, not just to two unlucky parents.

Graves at St James church, Cooling.

The beach at Shellness, at the east side of the Isle of Sheppey, was so named because it was entirely composed of tiny shells. Over time, the shells have been covered by sand and mud, and the area is most famous for hosting a naturist beach.

SHIP MONEY: SARRE HAS TO PLEAD POVERTY

As an important member of the Cinque Port Confederation, Sandwich had several 'daughter' ports called 'limbs' supporting it, which were Deal, Ramsgate, Brightlingsea (in Essex), Fordwich, Sturry, Walmer, Stonar, Sarre, St Nicholas and Reculver.

The importance of the Cinque Ports has been reduced by the advent of the Royal Navy, but some traditions remain, and each year the three remaining limb ports are called to Sandwich Guildhall. As they no longer provide Ship Service to the Confederation, they are allowed to give a sum of money as an alternative.

The Mayor Deputy of Brightlingsea is required to pay 10*s* (now worth approximately 50p) and the Mayor Deputy of Fordwich gives 3*s* and fourpence (now worth about 17p). The Mayor Deputy of Sarre traditionally pleads poverty and is exempt from paying.

It is not clear how long this tradition can continue as the value of the payment continues to reduce, but 1,000 years of history are not easily wiped out, even if all parties end up pleading for exemption.

THE SHIP ON SHORE: WASTE NOT, WANT NOT

The Ship on Shore pub in Sheerness has a curious construction in its car park that is hard to explain: it looks like a building made from barrel-shaped concrete blocks.

The story goes as follows: a ship carrying barrels of concrete was shipwrecked nearby in 1848 and the landlord raced to salvage the cargo, hoping for a valuable windfall. Finding that it was concrete and had already solidified, he decided not to waste the materials and built a folly from the blocks.

The grotto has outlasted many other buildings in the area made of less durable materials, and has been granted protected status as a Grade II listed building. Perhaps the landlord did strike it rich, after all.

The Ship on Shore pub, Sheerness.

THE SILKWORMS OF LULLINGSTONE CASTLE: THEY MADE THE ROYAL WEDDING AN AFFAIR TO REMEMBER

The silk farm in Lullingstone was established in the 1930s, and provided silk for the Coronation Robes in 1937 and for the gown of the Queen Mother worn at the event. The Princess who was destined to become Queen Elizabeth II chose to have her wedding dress made of Lullingstone silk, of which the farm is understandably very proud.

Although the silk farm has now moved, local people remember that almost every room in the castle was given over to silk production, and an annual blessing service was held at the local church at which the silkworms as well as the tools of the trade were blessed by the vicar.

SIX POOR TRAVELLERS: LIVING ON THE CHARITY OF OTHERS

The Six Poor Travellers' House in Rochester was built in 1586. The charity was founded by local MP Richard Watts, who left money in his will for the benefit of six poor travellers or wayfaring men, each of whom, according to a plaque on the outside of the building, would be given free lodging and 'entertainment' for one night before being sent on his way with fourpence in his pocket.

The house was added to an existing almshouse that gave training to pauper children and continued to provide service to poor travellers until the Second World War. It is interesting to note that those accepted could not be 'rogues' nor 'proctors' (a person begging by proxy for someone else), and also that the house was used by Charles Dickens as the inspiration for his collection of stories *The* Seven *Poor Travellers*.

The charity grew, expanded, and now provides accommodation for those in need on a long-term basis.

SLIPPERY SAM: AN OWLER FROM PETHAM

Smuggling was once rife in Kent, as the county had easy access to other countries by numerous sea routes. Smugglers carried wool, lace, spirits and even men back and forwards across the English Channel. Coins were also in high demand in mainland Europe – one legend tells of guineas being hidden in jars of pitch and bought at a general sale once they had crossed the water. If the price was right, they were willing to take a chance.

One of the most notorious smugglers was Slippery Sam. Sam was born in Petham, to the west of Canterbury, into a family of smugglers, so it was almost inevitable that he followed the family trade. He soon became involved with the Hawkhurst Gang, becoming an 'owler', as smugglers were known on the Romney Marsh.

His speciality was receiving and passing on goods, although he did sometimes join the smuggling runs. He was given his nickname after a daring escape from Maidstone Jail, during which he smeared his body with grease so he could escape through a narrow window.

He met his fate in 1760, when he killed a Revenue Officer and was hanged for the offence, at just 30 years old.

SMACK BOYS: WORKING ON THE FISHING SMACKS OF NORTH KENT

The Smack Boys Home in Ramsgate is an example of a charity for fishing apprentices, opened as a sister institution to the Sailor's Church and Harbour Mission nearby.

Built in 1881, the home was run for the benefit of boys who worked on the fishing smacks of the area, which could amount to as many as four boys per boat. Fifty boats were registered in 1863, a number that had trebled by the end of the century, and when on shore the boys were often left without shelter; the home offered them refuge.

The home changed its remit in 1915 to offer help to sailors of all ages, but still bears the inscription *The Ramsgate Home for Smack Boys.*

SMALLEST PUB IN THE COUNTRY: ONLY SIX AT A TIME, PLEASE!

The Little Prince pub in Margate is 11ft long and just over 6ft wide – no bigger than the average box room, and yet it has claimed a big title. Located in the Old Kent Market in the town's conservation area, the Little Prince is the smallest pub in the UK, with room for just half a dozen customers at a time.

SQUIRREL BUNTING: A GOOD THING GONE BAD

Hasted reports that there was a strange custom carried out in Eastling and the surrounding villages known as squirrel bunting, during which the 'lower kind of people' came together to form a 'lawless rabble'.

Squirrel bunting took place on St Andrew's Day (30 November) each year, and may once have been a means of keeping vermin in check. By the time Hasted wrote his survey of Kent in 1798, it had degenerated into a cruel and unnecessary day of rioting.

Armed with a variety of weapons, the group would spend hours in the woods, purportedly hunting squirrels, but also killing any hares or game birds they found, destroying woodlands, hedges and fences as they went, before ending up at the nearest pub.

Local opposition to this custom soon won the day, and squirrel bunting no longer takes place in Eastling or any other place in Kent.

STAPLEHURST BAPTISMS: UNCOMMON PRACTICES, COMMON IN KENT

The parochial records of Staplehurst have survived in remarkably good condition, not least because the Elizabethan practise of rewriting records made during the Roman Catholic rule of Mary I was not carried out.

One of the many peculiarities of the records is the amount of detail recorded, including the names of godparents and the names of those women brought to be 'churched' or cleansed after the birth of a child. Unusually, the names of stillborn children are also recorded, along with dispensations for those who were ill to be allowed to eat meat during the fasting season of Lent.

Keen genealogists will know the frustration of finding that many people in a family were baptised with the same name, but those researching Staplehurst families will also find such information as 'infant, child, youth, lad, wench, maiden, an old innocent man, a poor old maiden, a poor old wench, a poor old man with a stiff leg, an honest wife, full of alms and good works; an honest man, and good house holder; an honest matron', etc.

Lastly, the records show that many children were baptised by a 'woman of good report', rather than a member of the clergy. This refers to the practice of baptising babies that are unlikely to survive as soon as they are born. *The*

Beauties of England and Wales by John Britton, written in the early nineteenth century, puts forward the view that children were sometimes baptised even before they were born; this is a disputed practice that maintains that a child can be baptised if the water touches its head, for example during a Caesarean birth or while it is 'crowning'.

The records also show an amazing number of babies baptised under the name 'Creature', which seems to be a peculiarity of the Weald of Kent and Sussex, although the practice does spread further across the country. The name is a shortening of the term 'Creature of Christ', and is not meant to infer abnormality.

STONE ME! STREET NAME HONOUR FOR KENT'S MOST FAMOUS BAND

Dartford is rightly proud of Mick Jagger and Keith Richards, of the Rolling Stones, and the Mick Jagger Arts Centre was opened in 2000 by HRH Duke of Kent. Many people won't realise, however, that the band is also recognised in the street names of a new housing development. The council chose thirteen band-related street names and residents now have addresses in Little Red Walk, Cloud Close, Tumbling Dice Mews and Sympathy Vale, among others.

THE STREET: HOW THE PEOPLE OF TANKERTON CAN WALK ON WATER

The Street is one of the peculiarities of the north Kent coast. This entirely natural shingle strip has built up over the years, extending out into the sea from the shoreline at Tankerton. At low tide, this allows walkers to travel on dry land for half a mile with water either side of them. Formed by the peculiar drift of the local currents, The Street is unique in the British Isles.

SUBBUTEO: A KENTISH GAME

Peter Adolph from Langton Green had plenty of time to spare when he left the RAF. He used it to finalise plans for a game of table football he named Subbuteo, which he later sold to Waddingtons for £250,000. However, Kent remained home to Subbuteo until the early 1980s, when manufacturing moved to Leeds.

The Street, Tankerton.

SUSANNAH LOTT: LUCKY TO BE HANGED

In 1769, Susannah Lott was accused of being an accomplice in the murder of her husband, and was sentenced to be burnt to death. This was due to a vagary in the law at the time that stated a woman who murdered her husband was guilty of treason, and the punishment for treason was to be burnt at the stake.

Susannah's husband John was significantly older than her, and although she had never wanted to marry him, her boyfriend Benjamin Buss reasoned that if she married John, he would soon die and then she would inherit his not inconsiderable wealth. When Benjamin suggested they poison John to hasten his end, Susannah was initially reluctant, but did eventually agree.

John died, but the two were arrested and sentenced to death. Luckily for Susannah, somebody decided that the punishment was too harsh, and she was hanged on the stake before her body was burnt, saving her the agony of that fate. Twenty years later, death by burning was banned by Parliament.

T

TEMPTED BY A TUDOR: A LONELY QUEEN, HER LOVER, AND THE FUTURE KING OF ENGLAND

Legend has it that the widowed wife of Henry V, Catherine de Valoise, met and married Owain Tudor while living at Leeds Castle. The castle, named after Ledian, the Chief Minister of Ethelbert II, was a favourite home of the dowager Queen Catherine, who was only 21 at the time of her husband's death, and it is suggested that she started an affair with Owain Tudor while at Leeds when he was working as Clerk of her Wardrobe. Despite the difference in their status, they later married, and although she was initially stripped of her assets by her son, Henry VI, he repented and returned them before his death. As Henry VI left no heirs, the grandson of Catherine and Owain became Henry VII.

THANINGTON MURDER: A SUICIDE PACT THAT ENDED IN TRAGEDY

On 29 March 1929 two very ill young people were found in a field in Thanington, just outside Canterbury. They were taken to the Kent and Canterbury Hospital and although the young woman was found to be dead on arrival, the young man survived.

The police investigated, and found that the man was Ralph Pattison, a 31-year-old miner from Durham, and that the young woman, Margaret Dawson, was from Sunderland. It transpires that they had fallen in love and run away because Ralph was already married, but feeling that the situation was hopeless they had agreed on a suicide pact. Accordingly, they had both drunk a quantity of antiseptic disinfectant solution and been poisoned.

Ralph was brought to trial, and it was found that he was guilty of the crime of murder, as he had assisted in Margaret's death. He was initially given a death sentence, but this was commuted to penal servitude for life, which, considering the circumstances of the crime, might have been a much worse punishment to bear.

THEFT OF AN ORNAMENT: AN UNDIAGNOSED KLEPTOMANIAC

The *Folkestone Chronicle* of January 1862 follows the trial of William Hart, who was charged with stealing a chimney ornament worth just 1*s* from a local pub, where he had been working.

The policeman who arrested Hart said that he had gone to his house and found the ornament on the mantelpiece there. Hart pleaded guilty.

The Mayor, who was conducting the investigation, remembered that this was Hart's third offence of this kind. He said that although the proper punishment was three months in gaol, he would allow the more lenient punishment of two months' hard labour. He further added that if Hart was convicted again, he would be 'so dealt with as not to trouble the borough for some time'.

Reading between the lines, it seems that William Hart had a problem of some kind, in that he repeatedly stole small items without trying to hide them afterwards, and that he was given a light sentence. We will never know the story of William Hart, apart from this small insight into his world, but we can only hope he was not dealt with harshly.

THOMAS MORE'S HEAD: IN A REAL PICKLE

Sir Thomas More was Lord Chancellor at the time of Henry VIII and a personal friend of the king. However, he was a staunch Catholic, and could not agree with Henry's divorce from Katherine of Aragon, nor his insistence that he could become the Supreme Head of the Church in England.

More was put into the Tower of London and later executed. His head was placed on a spike on London Bridge, where it stayed for several weeks. When it was taken down, his daughter Margaret Roper, who lived in Canterbury, bribed the guard and took the head.

Thomas More's head, before it was relocated.

The Roper's house was in St Dunstan's, just opposite the church, and although the house is now long gone, the gate still remains, surrounded by a Tudor brick frontage, an impressive reminder of the family's wealth and importance.

To preserve the head, it is said that Margaret pickled it in spices and carried it in a lead-lined box to her home, where it stayed until after her death. A gruesome keepsake indeed.

The head is now said to rest in the Roper family vault in St Dunstan's church, just metres from the family home, while his headless body lies in an unmarked grave in the Tower of London.

TOAD IN THE HOLE: A PUB GAME WITH A DIFFERENCE

Once popular in the southern parts of Kent, the game of Toad in the Hole has now all but disappeared. This might be due to the fact that a special table was required, whereas other games, such as Shove Ha'penny, could be played on any table. The Toad in the Hole table was about the size of a single old-style school desk, with a hole in the middle. Players threw brass 'toads' or tokens at the table, from a pre-arranged distance, and the player who got the most in the hole won the game. Sometimes these simple games were the ones that required most skill.

TRADITIONAL TOYS: CANTERBURY – THE SINDY CITY

Although not invented in Kent, local people know that the Hornby factory has a visitor centre in Westwood, near Margate, and is a treasure trove of bargains and collectables.

However, even local people may not remember that Sindy, the British girl-next-door rival to siren Barbie, was at one time made in Canterbury. Invented by the Lines brothers in London, a factory was set up in Market Way, Canterbury, and was open from the late Sixties to the early Eighties producing the iconic doll.

TREACLE MINES AND MINERS: A CUSTOM THAT HAS STUCK AROUND

Only half a dozen counties in the UK claim to have treacle mines, and Kent is one of them. Supposedly dreamt-up by an enterprising Frittenden man hoping to draw in wealthy tourists from London, the myth persists, and Kent now purports to have mines at Tudeley and Tovil as well as Frittenden.

The Seven Champions Molly Dancers have based their style on that from sides further north, but their website states that they are, at heart, treacle miners: their high steps originate from wading through treacle and the strings around their trousers were originally to keep the treacle rats from running up their legs.

U

UNCONQUERED: THE MEANING OF KENT'S MOTTO

After the Norman invasion of 1066 the Norman troops raped and pillaged their way from Hastings, across Romney Marsh to Dover and up through Kent to London for William I's coronation.

Turning southwards again, William and his troops headed for Dover, but he had not counted on the resistance of the people of Kent. He was stopped at Swanscombe, by Stigande the Archbishop of Canterbury and Egelsine, the Abbot of St Augustines, where they battled for three days. Eventually, William saw that he was unlikely to win and negotiated a settlement. Kent became a County Palatine administered by William's half-brother Odo, Bishop of Bayeux, and as such remained unconquered by the Normans. The Kentish motto to this day is *Invicta* (Unconquered).

THE UPCHURCH INTRUDER: AN AUDACIOUS CRIME THAT WENT UNPUNISHED

We are advised these days to beware of opportunists, taking advantage of unlocked doors and windows, but this is not a new crime, as shown by a report in the *Kentish Weekly Post* in 1819.

At 11 p.m. one Sunday night in March of that year a man broke into the Royal Oak public house in Upchurch. Looking around and perhaps finding nothing of interest, he went upstairs to the room where the landlord and his wife were sleeping. They were woken up when they heard the intruder opening their chest of drawers. Startled, he ran off, but it was not until he had gone that they realised that he had taken a silver watch from near the head of the bed.

Sadly, the watch was never recovered.

THE VELOCIPEDE: PRECURSOR TO THE BICYCLE

Willard Sawyer became known throughout the world in the middle of the nineteenth century as the first professional maker of a man-powered vehicle.

By 1841, Sawyer had set up a workshop and a factory in St James Street, Dover, for the manufacture of the vehicle that was a precursor to the bicycle, although his design had four wheels, not two. The velocipede was stable enough to be used by ladies, children or invalids and he even produced a model large enough to carry a whole family at once.

The velocipede featured in the Great Exhibition at Crystal Palace in 1851, and the Emperor of Russia placed an order, as well as the Prince of Wales, who visited the factory in Dover. As well as the health benefits, one of the selling points of the velocipede was the saving to be made on the cost of hiring horses for a short trip. Eventually, the popularity of the velocipede was overtaken by that of the penny-farthing bicycle, and Sawyer's name is now all but forgotten.

A VIKING LONGSHIP AT PEGWELL BAY: A REMINDER OF OLD ENEMIES AND NEW FRIENDS

Visitors travelling south from Thanet on the Sandwich Road may be surprised to see a full-sized Viking ship perched on the cliffs above Pegwell Bay.

A replica longship, the *Hugin*, commemorates the 1,500th anniversary of the Viking invasion of Britain. The original ship was rowed here by modern-day Danes in 1949, who observed authentic Viking conditions onboard apart from the one instrument they took with them, a sextant.

* I was on it when it landed at BROADSTAIRS

The Viking longship *Hugin* at Pegwell Bay.

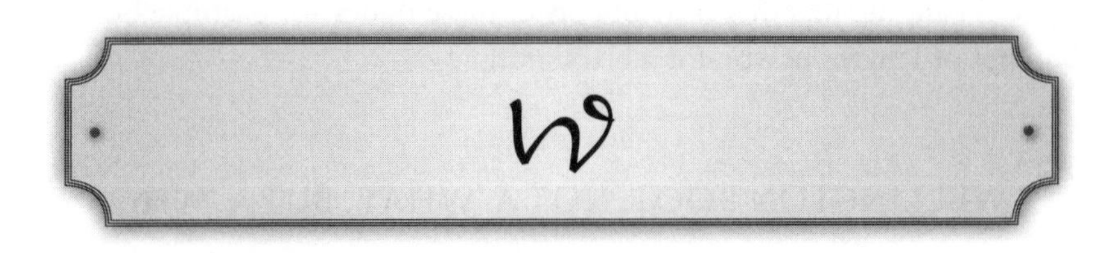

THE WAGHORN MEMORIAL: VIEW IT AT YOUR CONVENIENCE

The Waghorn Memorial in Chatham was erected in 1888 to the memory of Thomas Waghorn, who is remembered for finding an overland route to India fifty years earlier. He had negotiated a route through the deserts of Egypt and on to the Red Sea, thus halving the time of the three-month journey for passengers, post and trade goods.

One hand of the statue was intended to point out the route to interested visitors; sadly, it points in the wrong direction. The memorial should have been erected so that the extended hand pointed east, but instead it points north, to the public toilets. The reasons for this are myriad, but include the fact that this was not the intended location for the statue and the fact that, in this orientation, visitors are presented with a front view rather than a back view of the statue when exiting the railway station.

WEDDING TRADITIONS: STRANGE CUSTOMS IN CRANBROOK

Alfred Dunkin wrote, in 1855, about a strange custom in the village of Cranbrook.

Instead of flowers being laid outside the church for the bride and groom to walk upon, the local tradition was for articles relating to the trade of the bridegroom to be used. Thus, a carpenter and his new wife could expect to walk on wood shavings, or a cobbler upon leather. Bizarrely, this custom was extended to most unlikely occupations: a blacksmith might have some old iron for the couple to stumble over, and the bride of a butcher might be expected to walk across the skins of slaughtered sheep.

Dunkin also tells us that in other parts of Kent 'Rough Music' is provided by guests banging together instruments of these trades, for example bones for a butcher or lengths of iron for a blacksmith.

WELLINGTON BOOT: NOT A 'WHAT', BUT A 'WHO'

The people of Kent have an affinity with Wellington boots, often citing the fact that the Duke of Wellington, Lord Warden of the Cinque Port Confederation, was often in residence at Walmer Castle, and that you can see a pair of his original Wellington boots at the castle when you visit.

Not so many people know that William Wellington Boot was in fact a person who lived in the little village of Hawkinge on the south coast. William was born in 1904 and died in 1972, at the age of 68. His gravestone omits the name William and cites his name as 'Wellington Boot', by which he was probably known all his life.

A WEREWOLF IN ASHFORD: A MODERN-DAY FABLE BY SUTHERLAND MENZIES

The Victorians loved a bit of melodrama, and Elizabeth Stone knew this. She was a Victorian herself, and was well aware of the public taste for the gothic, and so created *Hugues the Wer-Wolf*, writing under the name Sutherland Menzies.

The story is set in Kent, and the Wulfric family live between Ashford and Canterbury, inhabiting a wooded stretch of land between the two towns. Indeed, the modern-day traveller will still pass a dark stretch of woodland on the present-day A28, and it is not hard to believe that werewolves still live in the area. We wonder if Elizabeth, writing in 1838, created the story from her imagination, or whether she had heard whispers from the local people, as she suggests. Perhaps such creatures still lurk in the wilder areas of Kent, of which there are many. (*See* also Big Cats, The Great Dogg of Trottiscliffe.)

WEST MALLING WORKHOUSE: INSPIRATION FOR A MASTERPIECE

Kent is well-known for its association with writers such as Charles Dickens, Siegfried Sassoon and H.E. Bates, along with countless others who visited the area, such as Sir Arthur Conan Doyle and Ian Fleming.

One writer who travelled to Kent and used his experiences in his writing was Wilfred Owen. Owen travelled to Kent in the 1930s and stayed in West Malling workhouse while looking for work. He eventually found work as a farmhand and used both these experiences to inspire *Down and Out in Paris and London* and the *Hop Picking Diaries*.

WESTGATE TOWERS: PLACE OF EXECUTION

Canterbury Gaol was once housed in Westgate Towers, the only remaining gate through the old city walls, and it was here that prisoners were held and often executed.

The Newgate Chronicles tell us the story of Margaret Hughes, hanged from the towers on 4 July 1799 for murdering her husband by poisoning him. A special platform was rigged up for the event about 10 feet from the ground upon which were the gallows. This was on the north side of the towers, so as to be outside the city walls.

She was led up onto the platform and on the stroke of 1 p.m. the trap door was released and she fell to her death, hanged from the neck. It is noted in the report that the drop, a 'short drop', was only 6–8 inches, which was quite often not enough to break the victim's neck, and they would have been strangled to death. This was later replaced by using the system of a 'long drop', which was more humane. She was left for one hour, to ensure she was dead, before the body was taken down and sent for dissection (*see* Bodysnatchers).

WHELK BOATS AND WHERRIES: A BOAT FOR ALL SEASONS

Kent has a huge coastline, measuring almost 350 miles in length and covering a range of environmental conditions, from cliff faces to shingle and harbours to mudflats. Add to this the hundreds of miles of river that were once navigable and you will quickly realise that several different types of craft were required for the different conditions. The men who worked on the waterways and off the shores of Kent worked with many types of boat that were common elsewhere, but also devised their own styles to suit the conditions in which they worked.

The Medway doble was a fishing boat, which measured 18ft long and had a fish well in the middle. They were used in the lower parts of the River Medway, under sail or oar power.

Westgate Towers, Canterbury.

The Deal galley was a long, open boat with four or six oars, measuring up to 30ft in length. These ferried pilots to and from waiting vessels, who took over the ship and piloted it through the dangerous sandbanks to shore. Slightly smaller boats, known as galley punts were used for hovelling, a term particular to the east coast of Kent. Hovellers helped to rescue crew from stricken ships and also to remove cargo in a salvage operation.

The sailors of Dungeness faced difficulties before they even got their boats into the water. The wide shifting shingle beaches meant that permanent launch sites could not be constructed. The answer was a moveable caterpillar of oak planks, placed under the front of both fishing boats and lifeboats as they were pushed down into the water. Each plank had a rope attached and it was traditionally the women's job to tug each plank away from the back of the boat and place it in front, as the boat travelled towards the sea.

Deal luggers were larger than the galley, measuring perhaps 40ft in length, with a cabin to the fore. Some were fishing boats, but many were used in the same way that the galley punts were, taking provisions and passengers to and from ships waiting off shore. Their larger size meant they could carry more cargo.

Gravesend watermen's skiffs were a sturdier version of the boats used by the Thames watermen in London, made to stand up to the rougher conditions in the seas of the Thames Estuary.

Whitstable whelk boats were double-ended open boats, based on Norfolk whelk boats, but again made of sturdier construction to suit local conditions.

The Thanet wherry was a shallow beach boat and was originally for fishing, but as the tourist trade blossomed, many were pressed into service as pleasure craft, taking visitors on short trips out to sea.

WHITSTABLE OYSTER COMPANY: AN EARLY CO-OPERATIVE

Oysters have been harvested from the waters of the north Kent coast for thousands of years, and those from Whitstable have become famous throughout the world, growing in a ground protected by a shingle spit (*see* The Street) and fed by fresh water from the Kent marshes. The Whitstable Oyster Company was set up to protect the fishing stocks and the rights of its members as early as the fifteenth century, and has been in operation ever since.

In 1793, Thomas Foord bought the fishing rights to that area of the sea around Whitstable and set up the Company of Free Fishers and Dredgers of

Whitstable. The company was regulated by an Act of Parliament, and controlled the industry to such an extent that it even had its own Water Court to resolve disputes. At this time there were about seventy oyster smacks fishing the waters in the area. Oysters were sold in bushels, a measure equating to 8 gallons, and by 1823 were fetching 4 guineas a bushel at the Billingsgate market.

Whitstable Oyster Fishery Company was set up by another Act in 1896 when the company was sold on to investors, and each member of the old company was allowed twenty shares. Orders were telegrammed to the company from Billingsgate Fish Market in London, and the work was divided up amongst the crews of the oyster smacks. Profits were shared, sick pay was granted, and benefits were allowed to the widows and orphans of members when necessary. It is an interesting quirk of the company that the water bailiff carried, as his badge of office, a small oar, mirroring the mace or gubernaculum of the officer of the Cinque Port. (*See* Cinque Ports.)

Those fishermen working outside the Company waters were known as 'flatsmen', and they made a living dredging the public areas of the sea bed.

Whitstable Oyster Company, Whitstable.

WILLIAM OF PERTH: PATRON SAINT OF ADOPTED CHILDREN

William was a devout baker from Perth, Scotland, who was known for his good works, in particular taking in an orphaned boy and raising him as an apprentice. In 1201, William and his adopted son travelled south on their way to Jerusalem. Sadly, William was murdered by the ungrateful apprentice near Chatham and his body was left by the wayside; he had suffered a blow to the head before his throat was cut.

His corpse was discovered by a woman who lay a garland of flowers on the body before changing her mind and placing the garland on her own head. She claimed she was instantly cured of her previous madness and William was buried in Rochester Cathedral with full honours. The miracles continued, and over the next fifty years the shrine became famous throughout the country, second in importance to the Thomas à Becket shrine at nearby Canterbury. William was canonised in 1256 and thus became a saint.

William's shrine was so popular, that a one-way route in and out of the cathedral was put into place. Pilgrims would be rerouted from Watling Street through Black Boy Alley, through St William's Gate to the door and into the north transept. Tradition demanded that they approach the shrine on their knees, and the constant brushing of cloth on stone left a permanent mark on the staircase. Having finished their devotions, visitors were ushered out through the south transept.

Although the shrine was destroyed in 1538 on the orders of King Henry VIII, and William's following diminished, a thirteenth-century wall painting depicting him was discovered in 1883 in Frindsbury church, Strood. The bearded figure of St William is depicted as a pilgrim and holding a bag and staff. Despite the fact that he was treated so abominably by his own adopted son, he is now the patron saint of adopted children.

WINDING PONDS: STATIONARY ENGINES FOR AN EMERGING RAILWAY SYSTEM

Kent was the site of one of the first commercial railway lines, running between Canterbury and the little seaside village of Whitstable. The line was opened in 1830, giving Canterbury access to the River Thames.

The first steam engine to carry cargo and passengers the 7 miles between the two towns was the *Invicta*, designed by Robert Stevenson. Sadly, the engine could not cope with the three steep hills along the route and stationary winding engines were installed to haul the train to the top. The water for the engines was supplied from specially constructed 'winding ponds'. The pond near Tyler's Hill has been restored and is now a picnic site, accessible from the Crab and Winkle Way, a footpath following the line of the railway using the nickname of the line.

WISTERIA: RECORD-BREAKING PLANTS IN THE GARDEN OF ENGLAND

With a reputation for being the Garden of England, it should come as no surprise that the oldest wisteria in England is said to be that at Chilham Castle, with the second oldest covering the walls of the West Garden in Canterbury Cathedral grounds.

WITCH TRIALS: HOW TO FIND OUT WHICH WITCH IS WHICH

Witch trials were carried out at the beginning of the 1450s across England. Luckily, the men and women of Kent suffered far less than those in other counties, notably Essex.

Witch trials started in the middle of the fifteenth century and lasted for almost 200 years, with the highest number of accusations falling in the 1640s. Many women were falsely accused, and many who sat in judgement saw sense and gave lenient punishments. However, many women and some men did perish, to our shame.

Although some of the more horrific forms of torture were soon banned in Britain, the use of starvation diets and sleep deprivation continued, along with the popular use of the ducking stool for 'swimming'. A woman accused of being a witch was tied to a stool and pushed into water. If she floated, she was guilty, as it was believed that the Devil was saving her. If she sank, she was innocent, but usually dead.

Ducking stools can still be seen in Kent, one in Canterbury and one in Fordwich. Luckily, they no longer function as a means of ascertaining guilt or innocence.

The Witchcraft Act of 1735 stopped the capital punishment of witches, but the Mayor of Sandwich still carries a staff of blackthorn as part of his regalia, which is a traditional charm against their magic.

WOOLWICH IN ESSEX: A TOWN DIVIDED

We all know that London is gradually swallowing up the suburbs that lie around it, but a little-known fact is that from the Norman Conquest until 1888, North Woolwich, situated on the northern banks of the River Thames, was administered as part of Kent, and was variously known as North Woolwich, Woolwich in Essex or even Kent in Essex.

The town of Woolwich had been granted to the Sheriff of Kent by William the Conqueror, and it seems that he extended the lands he held as far as he could. Many towns have a river running through the middle, so he could see no reason why Woolwich should be any different, and it was particularly valuable to him to hold land on both sides of the Woolwich Ferry.

The land is now part of east London, but it is curious to think that the land boundaries differed so much that they crossed the great River Thames.

WORLD CUSTARD PIE CHAMPIONSHIP: A LITTLE BIT OF MADNESS IN THE KENTISH COUNTRYSIDE

Inspired by the antics of comedian Charlie Chaplin, the World Custard Pie Championships have been held at Coxheath, near Maidstone, each year since 1969. Teams of four compete in a championship of complete hilarity, and points are awarded by the judges. With fancy dress costumes and dripping custard, this is a family day out that shows the lighter side of the Kentish character.

THE EXPORT OF FLINTS AND FLINTLOCKS: AN INTERNATIONAL TRADE

As any Kentish gardener knows, the chalky soil is full of flint. Once so useful to the craftsmen of the Palaeolithic era, the flints became useful once again during the age of early firearms. For almost two centuries, from the seventeenth onwards, a regular supply of flints was needed for the flintlock guns in use across the country and by the armies at home and overseas.

Once mined, flint was dried and then napped into flakes before being worked into the wedged square shape of the gun flint. Flints were made in varying sizes to fit the different guns from musket to pistol. Kent was

A Brown Bess flintlock carbine.

renowned for the quality of its gun flints, giving rise to a brisk export trade, which ceased in the early nineteenth century when production moved almost wholly to East Anglia.

Flint was also used as a building material, and flint knappers are still in demand for restoration work, as many buildings in Kent are fortified against the elements with an outer layer of knapped flint.

YALDING'S TEAPOT ISLAND: A TINY ISLAND WITH A HUGE COLLECTION

As the River Medway dips under the B2162 near Yalding, a tiny island has formed, which is now home to 7,600 teapots. Once a tiny café serving the local fisherman, this amazing and truly unique visitor attraction now appears in the *Guinness Book of World Records* and welcomes thousands of visitors a year. How very English!

YANTLET LINE: DIVIDING THE RIVER FROM THE SEA

During the Early and Middle Ages, the King of England owned the fishing rights for every river in the country, including those that ran through London. When King Richard I found himself short of cash in 1197, he sold his sovereign rights over part of the River Thames to the City of London. The extent of the new jurisdiction was duly marked with stone posts, in Staines (Middlesex) to the west, Upnor to the south, as the river merges with the River Medway, and Yantlet, on the Isle of Grain, and Crowstone (Essex) to the east. Giant stone obelisks, known as London Stones, were erected at each location, and visited annually in a ceremonial visit by the authorities. The weathered stones were replaced several times, most recently in 1836, and although the jurisdiction of the City of London ceased a few years later, the Kentish stones still remain in situ. The older of the two stones at Lower Upnor is dated 1204 and has the inscription 'God preserve the City of London'.

The imaginary line drawn across the mouth of the river between Kent and Essex became known as the Yantlet Line, delineating the limit of the authority of the Port of London Authority. Without this marker, the tiny hamlet of

Yantlet would have remained in obscurity, whereas now it is known by every waterman who sails on the Thames.

YELLOW-TAILED SCORPIONS: 10,000 SCORPIONS THAT GLOW IN THE DARK

The yellow-tailed scorpion is tiny, measuring just 2in long, but can still give a nasty sting to an unwary human. You might consider that you are unlikely to see one in Kent, but you would be mistaken.

Having hitched a lift on trading ships from warmer waters, the scorpions came ashore at Britain's ports, and although a few small colonies have established themselves around the south coast, none is as large nor as old as that on the Isle of Sheppey.

The scorpions have been on the Island for at least 200 years, having made their home in the sun-warmed walls of the dockyard at Sheerness, and it is now estimated that there are over 10,000 of them, living in the cracks and crevices of the brickwork.

Yellow-tailed scorpion.

On a warm day, it is quite possible to see the scorpions in broad daylight, but a trip out at night-time will show their numbers as, like all scorpions, they glow green under UV light.

YOULING AND WASSAILING: ENSURING A GOOD CROP FOR THE COMING YEAR

The word 'wassail' derives from the Germanic words *waes hail* meaning 'be healthy', brought to Kent by Hengist and his family. Apple Wassailing takes place in January, in the hope of ensuring a good crop of cider apples at the next harvest. As the apple trees lie dormant in winter, one lucky tree in each orchard is doused with the previous year's cider. Whether the original ceremony was devised as an offering, a reminder of what is expected, or just a wake-up call is no longer recalled, but the practice not only continues, but is growing in popularity.

Modern examples of the tradition include the evening celebrations at The Gate Inn, Marshside, to which the re-enactment group of the 3rd East Kent Regiment are invited, so they can continue the tradition of firing into the trees, adding to the noise of drums being banged, to scare away evil spirits. The event includes the traditional libation of the trees and communal drinking from the wassail cup, and is often attended by Hoodeners or Morris sides.

Edward Hasted recalls that a similar custom to wassailing took place in early summer in West Wickham, in the far west of the county. The ceremony took place on Rogation Day at the end of April, just as the fruit was setting, but the practice has sadly now been discontinued or subsumed by the May festivities.

From Hasted's recollection, young men encircled one tree in the orchard, and with much noise and hilarity, recited the following poem:

Stand fast root, bear well top;
God send us a YOULING sop!
E'ry twig, apple big;
E'ry bough, apple enow!

When they had finished, the custom was for the orchard owner to offer them a drink or a small donation. However, if the landowner refused, both he and his trees were loudly cursed by the youths.

Z

ZOO IN A PUB: MEDWAY'S FIRST ZOO

The Fenn Bell Inn near St Mary Hoo, half a dozen miles north of Rochester, was once well-known for being in the middle of nowhere. The isolated spot was in the tiny hamlet of Fenn Street, consisting of just a few cottages and The Bell public house. Legend has it that the bell in question was one of several used to help travellers find their way across the desolate, unlit marshes.

The current owners have developed a brisk trade, and created a licenced zoo within the grounds. Visitors can see rescued monkeys, meerkats, parrots, raccoons, lemurs and farm animals in what is now a tourist destination rather than a lonely outpost on the very edge of the county.

THE ZOMBIE APOCALYPSE: HOLLYWOOD COMES TO EAST KENT

The pharmaceutical giant Pfizer built up a research facility just outside the little town of Sandwich over a period of more than fifty years, so it was a sad day for the local economy when it closed in 2011, and an even bigger problem when the zombies moved in!

The site, known as the birthplace of Viagra, had scores of on-site offices, warehouse and science labs. To maintain secrecy about activities on the site visitors were signed in, transported in company cars, and required to leave their mobile phones at reception. The year after Pfizer moved away, however, theatre-goers across the globe were treated to a trip around the site, seeing it not as part of the Pfizer empire, but as the laboratories where scientists, led by actor Brad Pitt, were trying to find a cure for a zombie pandemic.

Pitt's then-wife Angelina Jolie joined the star in Kent while he was filming, staying with their family in Ickham, a village to the east of Canterbury, visiting in a typical Kentish pub, and shopping in the village store. In this instance, Kent didn't go to Hollywood – Hollywood came to Kent!

Conclusion

The county of Kent has a history longer than most and over time has accrued many traditions whose origins are lost in time.

We have also grown our fair share of explorers, mystics and eccentrics, who have created fascinating buildings and inspired magnificent monuments to themselves and their achievements.

With some of the most beautiful countryside in the UK and a rich playbook of festivals, Kent is an attractive destination for the day traveller. But those who delve deeper will find an almost inexhaustible pool of legends and mysteries; pore over books, visit the museums, and you will soon find that a study of the culture of Kentish Man could take you a lifetime.

Kentish hop flowers.